What People Are Saying

"Kim Harms is a hero. And I can't say that about many people I have known. We've had the opportunity to capture her story in digital interviews with Kim and her husband Jim, and there are few who have faced pain and suffering like the Harms, but yet Kim keeps her eyes above, and God is using her heartbreaking story to now help others with the wisdom she has gained through tragedy. *"Are You Ready? How to Build a Legacy to Die For"* is a well-thought-out story and a blueprint for how we can love our families, and our neighbors well with the short time we all have been given in our earthly bodies. She is absolutely correct in her cultural observation that we will go to extremes to extend our lives by 1 day, 1 month, 1 year, etc., rather than taking the time to thoughtfully look at our legacy and what simple steps we can take now to provide a legacy plan for our loved ones after we are gone. I highly recommend this book for all of us and as a wonderful gift for a friend. What is your legacy going to be?"

—Steve Johnson

Multiple Emmy Award winning producer, executive director and co-founder, Five Stone Media, and LifeSupport Resources

"This book is a must read for all ages. It contains important ideas that should be considered by everyone wanting to ensure that family and friends understand their intentions No greater legacy can be left."

—Dr. Sheryl Ramstad, JD, DNP, MN, RN

"Don't read this book! Unless you want to Be READY! Kim's riveting account of stories will captivate you and make you think. It was hard to put the book down. It's packed full of resources that will prepare you and your family for end of life and the legacy you want to build now! As my husband, Ron Black, said before his death. You die well by living well today!"
—Kathy B. Dempsey, RN, MED, CSP, author of *Shed or You're Dead®*

"Kim weaves her dramatic life story with expert advice on living your best life and sharing it with close family and generations to come.
You'll be glad you read it as you build your legacy."
—Lindsay Strand, former television journalist, consultant and real estate professional

"*Are You Ready? How to Build a Legacy to Die For* is a must-read so that we better understand how we are building our legacy step-by-step, person-by-person, year-by-year. She makes it clear we should not leave these important conversations until it is too late."
—Carol Rueppel, retired television executive

Are You Ready?

How to Build a Legacy to Die for

DR. KIMBERLY HARMS

Printed in the United States of America

Hardcover ISBN: 978-1-960876-17-1
Paperback ISBN: 978-1-960876-18-8
Ebook ISBN: 978-1-960876-19-5
Library of Congress Control Number: 2023944849

Muse Literary
3319 N. Cicero Avenue
Chicago IL 60641-9998

This book is dedicated as a legacy *from* my mother, Anna Mae McKiernan (Potts), my husband James Roger Harms, and my son Eric James Harms. It is also dedicated as a legacy *to* my living children, grandchildren, and extended family. I love them with all my heart.

Contents

Foreword

Are you going to die? Strange way to start a foreword to any book, I know that! But the reality is that some of us choose to "live" as though we were never "leaving!" We all will leave! Those of us who are believers in God's plan for our eternal life, will not "die," but live eternally with Him.

But we will leave this Earth! Isn't it strange that we don't really start thinking about "leaving a lasting legacy" until nearing life's end? When *really*, we have been building that legacy our entire life on this Earth. It is left behind us, but *as* important, it is *lived* as we experience life daily while we are here.

Warning: when you start reading this book, by the amazing Dr. Kim Harms, you will have a hard time putting it down! It is a powerful legacy of the importance of beginnings in our lives. Not just the actual "happenings" of our beginnings, but our choices in how we will respond to those beginnings. People who come from amazing backgrounds do not always choose to be amazing! People who come from very difficult backgrounds sometimes succeed in powerful/purposeful ways! The difference: *choice*! Yes, the familiar quote is: "It is not what happens to you, but what you do about it that makes all the difference!" Kim's beginnings were tragic in most ways...a blessing in many ways!

The blessings won! She pulls out of life laughter, hope, resilience, faith, courage, power, purpose, and passion! Kim's reflection (her legacy) is being lived through the healing professions/passions of dentistry, philanthropy, professional speaking, spiritual faith, world vision (leading to international travel and establishing libraries in honor of her son, Eric), marriage, family, friendship, and *writing*! I added "writing" last because this is the medium which we are privileged to hold in our hands, and take to our hearts to live "well" so that we leave "worthy lives!" I know you will read every word... I know you will choose to be and live different lives... I know you will choose to "leave" more powerful life legacies... And I *know* you will share this book with friends and loved ones! I can just hear you saying, "I just read a book about 'Living Our Legacy' by Dr. Kim Harms!"

Underline and take notes. You just must read it, re-read it, and recommend others to read it also!

—Naomi Rhode, CSP, CPAE, Speaker Hall of Fame, Global Speaking Fellow, past president National Speakers Association, past president Global Speakers Federation

Prologue

It was a very small card featuring a muted pink rose in full bloom. The inscription was simple: "All my love, always, Mom." There was a $5 bill inside, one-third of my mom's net worth. My sister Mindy and brother Mike received an identical card, each written shortly before my kind, loving, beautiful mother took her life away from us. I was seventeen. We lost her the first time when I was six, and she was institutionalized for what is now known as bipolar disease. We lost her the second time three months later when, after my dad refused to give us back to her, she collapsed into despair, and was institutionalized again. This time for life. The card was all that remained of her. Or so I thought.

Anything good I had become, I became because of my mother. She loved me unconditionally. She taught me I could do anything. She gave me my faith. Even though my life after six contained none of those affirmations, six years of love was enough to learn that I was enough. How lucky was I?

We are, all of us, going to die one day. Yet Americans live in a culture that denies death. We can hardly say the word. We work very hard to do everything possible to stay alive as long as possible, yet we do very little to prepare for what I believe is our most important job: to make ready those that we love to continue without us. Individuals well prepared will have their Last Will and Testament in place and provide a clear financial plan for their families. The even better prepared will have a Health Care Directive or Living Will in place to help guide their loved ones through their final days. Yet, how many of us leave a clear message to the most important people in our lives that we love them, we are proud of them, they are strong, and they are enough? I hope this book will serve as a guide to help assist our families and others important in our lives for the time when we are no longer physically able to comfort, love, and encourage them.

Introduction

We live in a chaotic, uncontrolled, and even scary world, but simultaneously beautiful, full of love, and joy. It is filled with people who are educated and uneducated, tall and short, colorful, beautiful, and nice or not so nice. There exists good and evil on our bewildering planet, and occasionally it is hard to know the difference. Some cultures live together and work together well, and some don't. There are wars, economic uncertainties, and global pandemics. There are also spectacular sunsets, dazzling beaches, and awe-inspiring rainforests.

Throughout this immense 197,060,800 square mile irregularly shaped ellipsoid (really–according to the National Oceanic and Atmospheric Administration, the earth is not exactly round), and for its eight billion (and counting) people, we all share two things. At some point, every one of us experienced the incredible miracle of birth, and at some point, we will also experience the ultimate certainty of death. This book is designed to help you make the maximum use of the time in between.

Part one of this book is devoted to examining affirmatory endowments you can leave behind, such as love, education, and a positive work ethic. You will meet incredible people who have left legacies of hope, resilience, and love that lasted multiple generations. Some of these stories will be hard to read as the greatest legacies and the greatest hopes are frequently born from horrific pain.

Part two looks at the process of death itself and your choices at the end of life. We will also explore some research on Near

Death Experiences (NDEs) and ask, "Is this life all there is for us?" with the understanding that beliefs on this topic differ.

Part three of this book focuses on getting ready to transition by leaving your loved ones prepared to move forward after you have died. We will provide a list of things you can do to help them take care of your affairs and also what you can do now to leave them as emotionally ready as possible to live without you.

Unfortunately, many of us wait until we have a terminal diagnosis before we start working on these tasks, which adds additional stress to an already stressful time. Why not get this out of the way now? Part three also explores the concept of legacy and gratitude letters, which can be written and sent today or included in your legacy folder to be delivered after your death. You are never too young to write a gratitude letter.

Consider this book a hardcopy, life-coaching plan focusing on ending well.

As Maya Angelou once said, "You have no idea what your legacy will be because your legacy is every life you touch."

Part One: Legacy

Your Life Is Your Legacy

There isn't time, so brief is life, for bickerings, apologies, heartburnings, calling to account. There is only time for loving, and but an instant, so to speak, for that.
—Mark Twain

Every legacy is unique to the individual. We are all shaped by the location of our birth, our parents' character, the time we are born, the faith (or lack thereof) in which we are born, the people we encounter, and our genetic idiosyncrasies. We learn as we grow, we experience joy and pain at different levels, and our sense of self is molded year over year by our interactions with those around us. The good news is that every one of us, no matter the personal circumstances we find ourselves in now, can pass on a positive legacy. We can also pass on the negative legacies of shame, toxic guilt, fear, anger, and low sense of self. These characteristics frequently start in childhood when our view of the world and our part in it is forming. Abuse, neglect, and harsh judgments of children can lead to adverse outcomes, such as mental illness or destructive behaviors, that last a lifetime. Our relationship with our spouse is modeled to our children, and our parenting style can sometimes be traced back to the legacy left by our parents.

One of the best examples of someone who transformed from leaving negative legacies such as crime and abandonment to positive legacies focused on helping wayward or absentee fathers fix themselves and their families is John Turnipseed (see Legacy of Mentorship). His book *Bloodline: You Spend Enough Time in Hell You Get the Feeling You Belong* is a must read for anyone caught in the trap of addiction or crime and in need of redemption.

No matter your history, tomorrow is another day. I am a firm believer in redemption. Every one of us has the potential to leave a positive legacy that is bigger than ourselves. We can start right now!

We can't change our past or our parents' pasts; we can only control the opportunities we have today to improve things. We are all capable of showing love and kindness to those around us, no matter the circumstances. We can also build a beautiful legacy for ourselves by cementing those positive virtues inwardly, into our own hearts. Creating a positive legacy is a phenomenal win-win situation for those who provide it and those who receive it.

Also, building legacies is best done without fanfare. Samuel Butler once said, "When you have told someone you have left him a legacy, the only decent thing to do is die at once." Don't die before your time; just build your legacy quietly! We leave a legacy with every action we take or do not take to every person we encounter.

Our legacy is shaped by our story and the stories of those who preceded us. This chapter tells my story. It starts before I was born.

Anna Mae McKiernan-Potts knew how to love. She was beautiful, she was funny, she was brilliant, and she was my mother. Mom was the youngest of five children and the only girl. Her mother, Grandma Fran, grew up in an upper-middle-class family but married a very handsome rogue (my grandfather) who drank. Since alcohol consumption and steady employment do not mix well, Grandpa could not keep a job, and Grandma had to work very hard when Mom was young. Grandpa was abusive and cruel to his family when he drank. Eventually, when the older boys were in their late teens and after a particularly brutal attack on Fran, the four boys kicked him out of the house. He never came back.

Mom grew up to be stunningly beautiful. She was often compared to Vivien Leigh, the famous English movie star at the time best known for her role as Scarlett O'Hara in *Gone with the Wind*. Mom had thick, dark, shoulder-length hair, full lips, and incredible deep-set, clear blue eyes. Mom also had lovely hands and even did some hand modeling. After high school, she worked as a telephone operator for Bell Telephone. A few years later, she was named Miss Bell Telephone, and off she went to ride the Bell Telephone Float at the Mardi Gras Parade in New Orleans, Louisiana.

As she was riding the float, she was spotted by a handsome recent graduate of the Naval Academy: my dad, Bobby Lee Potts. I don't know exactly how he tracked her down or the date they met, but sparks must have flown. They were married within the week. They say opposites attract.

Dad was handsome, athletic, and brilliant. He was an engineer, physicist, and highly practical. He grew up as one of three boys in Mexico, Missouri. His father, Grandpa Bill, ran a pool hall, and his mother, Grandma Alla, worked in a shoe factory. My grandparents were great role models for me and loved each other until the day Grandpa Bill died from a heart attack at age fifty-six.

Despite Dad's absences due to his naval career, my brother Mike was born into their marriage in 1952. His birth was followed by several miscarriages, which devastated my mother. I was born in 1956, followed thirteen months later by my sister Mindy. When Mom was pregnant with me, she, Dad, and Mike were traveling across the country from Virginia to California, as Dad was to attend the Naval Postgraduate School in Fort

Ord, California. We were moving to Carmel. On the way, they stopped in Mom's hometown of Cincinnati, Ohio. Mom was suffering from morning sickness. Her best friend, Jo, was also pregnant and told Mom of a fantastic new drug widely available in Europe but only being tested here in the US. A family member was involved in the testing, and Jo had been taking the new drug and thought it helped her. She gave Mom some tablets, and Mom also felt that they helped her feel better. That drug was thalidomide. My birth was traumatic as I came into the world with only seven fingers and some spinal abnormalities. Mom's friend Jo's baby was born severely deformed and died shortly after birth. They didn't find out why until years later.

After completing his courses at Ft. Ord, Dad was moved to Jacksonville on orders. It was there that the marriage between my parents broke down. Mom was beginning to show the initial stages of bipolar disease. The honing of a naval career at that time required a fine balance between achievement and social finesse. Mom's behavior was becoming an embarrassment to Dad. He could not cope. Being different was no longer attractive.

Mom, Grandma Fran, Mike, Mindy, and I moved back to Dad's hometown of Mexico, MO, and lived with our grandparents. Dad and Mom divorced in 1960 when I was three. Mom emotionally collapsed. She became suicidal but did not want her children scarred by the death of their mother. At one point, she stopped our car with Mike, Mindy, and me on a railroad track and waited for a train to come. Fortunately, Mike's screams alerted Mom to what she was doing, and she drove off before the train could hit us and soon entered a mental hospital in Missouri. For those ten minutes on the track, Mom was not being good mother. But for every minute of the rest of her life, she was a wonderful mother. She showed me unconditional love, taught me how to manage other people's reactions to my missing fingers, brought laughter into my life, and gave me the faith in God (please translate according to your belief system) that sustains me to this day.

Mental illness does not disqualify you from being a good parent. Lack of love does. Love is the greatest legacy. The love you leave lives on in those left behind. Any love that I have been able to show in my life is due to the love shown by my God and my mother.

When Mom was released from the hospital in Missouri, we moved to Cincinnati to be close to her family. We lived just down the street from my Uncle Tom and his family, including lots of cousins. Mom worked for my uncles, and Grandma Fran lived with us and took care of us during the day. Our home was a happy one.

Less than two years after the divorce, Dad married a navy nurse, Adrienne. He forgot, however, to tell Adrienne that he had three children. When she discovered this, he assured her that my mom had custody, so she wouldn't have to take care of us. Soon after the wedding, Adrienne became pregnant with her first child. In 1962, Dad discovered that the drug thalidomide, never approved for distribution in the US but used widely in Europe, was responsible for the disfigurement of approximately ten thousand babies. The babies were missing appendages (frequently born without arms and legs) and other congenital disabilities. Dad immediately called Mom, blaming her for my lack of fingers. Mom despaired, blaming herself. Shame and guilt took over. She couldn't cope with this news. She became despondent and severely depressed. Mom was admitted to Cincinnati's Mental Hospital within a week.

Dad picked us up and drove us to Maryland, where he lived in a two-bedroom duplex with Adrienne, now about four months pregnant. As soon as he dropped us off, he returned to his ship.

I can't imagine how Adrienne felt to have her life disrupted by being responsible for caring for three unexpected children, aged ten, six, and five, just as she was about to have her first child. She was not pleased and took her resentment out on us. Dad was not around.

Three months after entering the hospital, Mom was released. She asked Dad to bring us back; he said he couldn't because he had already bought the bedroom furniture. Mom, broken again, returned to the hospital and remained institutionalized for the rest of her life.

My father's life and career were about to be interrupted in another way by an international emergency.

Dad's goal was to become an admiral in the navy. One of the reasons he divorced my mom was that he was embarrassed by her mental illness. Adrienne, an attractive navy nurse, was much better suited to navy life. She knew the rules. Commanding a ship was one way to move up the ladder to admiral status. Dad had just been given his first command and then had it interrupted by a personal emergency (taking care of us). After dropping us off, he planned to continue that trajectory up the naval command ladder. Unfortunately, his climb up that ladder was again interrupted, permanently this time, by the Cuban missile crisis.

According to Dad, President Kennedy was appalled by the poor performance of the navy's surface-to-air missiles. He sent a strong message to the navy to collect their best engineers and physicists, bring them to the Pentagon, and improve the country's missiles. Dad was ordered to leave his ship and join this group. He was devastated. He considered working as a rocket scientist an obstacle to becoming an admiral. Dad served at the Pentagon for the rest of his navy career. He retired as soon as he was eligible, then worked for the Department of Commerce and as a consultant for the Booz Allen consulting firm. In the early days of computers, we had huge terminals filling our dining room that would connect by phone to a massive computer in a government building.

Dad then worked with friends to develop a computerized system for predicting the stock market called The BLP Forecast. That effort failed, and Dad blamed the failure on "outside forces" manipulating commodity prices. Finally, angry and embittered by life forces, he retired and bought a small resort on the Lake of the Ozarks in Missouri. He was still called back to DC as a consultant, working for Booz Allen, and claimed to have some input on the initial development of the Patriot missile. Dad died of a sudden heart attack at age fifty-six. I was twenty-five.

In Maryland, Mike, Mindy, and I pretty much grew up on our own. Adrienne and Dad were absent parents. One of the first things Dad said to us when we arrived was that the state required him to take care of us until we were eighteen but not to expect any help after that. Adrienne clearly did not like us, and we were second-class citizens in our own home. Mindy and Mike rebelled. Both left home in their middle teens. Mike, at age fourteen, stole a car with his friend. (I don't know how they learned to drive.) They tried to drive from Maryland to Cincinnati to find Mom. At a gas station in West Virginia, an attendant reported children driving a car. The two boys were picked up. Mike went to reform school after that, and Dad got him into the Merchant Marines. There was an attack on Mike's ship somewhere outside Vietnam, and he sustained abdominal injuries. Over thirty years later, Mike was a successful business-man, married with two beautiful daughters. A few days after a revision surgery due to the injuries suffered in the Merchant Marines, Mike had a heart attack and was the third man in our family to die at age fifty-six.

I am so proud of Mindy, who struggled for many years, but has become a successful hairdresser with an amazing daughter and a wonderful husband. And I remain close to my half-brother, Chris, and his lovely wife and children!

I was a conformist by nature and did well academically. When our father took custody of us, my mother made him promise to send us to Catholic school. It turned out to be a real blessing for me, but Mike and Mindy's rebellious behavior eventually had them expelled. I remained and graduated from Elizabeth Seton High School, an all-girls Catholic school in Bladensburg, MD. I was extremely shy and spent most lunch periods in the library. The Catholic, all-girl environment was helpful as there were fewer distractions. I loved my religion classes and truly felt that "God was in the building." Also, I loved basketball. I began high school two years before the passing of Title IX, which requires schools with public funding to offer girls sports. The Catholic schools had been offering girls sports for years, and when I was a junior, I made the team. Being on the team gave me some emotional status (even if it was only in my mind), and I got to wear the team mascot, a roadrunner, on my uniform. I started eating lunch because I felt I had a place at the table with my teammates. I was even assigned my own cheerleader. Everyone needs a cheerleader. My time in high school fostered the maturing of my faith and self-esteem. I will be forever grateful to my high school teachers.

I went on to attend the University of Maryland and claimed zoology as my major. I wanted to become a psychiatrist and save my mother from bipolar disease. Unfortunately, a month before I started college, Mom took her life away from us. I was devastated and depressed but understood the depths of pain and despair that would drive her to that decision. I had been there myself, and both Mindy and Mike had been there too.

During my first week of school, I was at a picnic hosted by the pre-professional groups on campus that included a softball game, and my team asked me to pitch. There was a cute guy on the other team; tall, blonde, with adorable John Lennon glasses.

He asked me out after the game. His name was Jim Harms. Jim would later recall that he hit three doubles off me and was able to check me out as he ran around the bases. I claimed that he struck out three times. Jim would retort that no one strikes out in slow-pitch softball. He was probably right.

Our first date was a university football game to which he invited my brothers Mark and Chris, who were in elementary school. He then took us to the barns at the college to show us how to milk the cows. Jim grew up on a farm with thirteen brothers and sisters. I fell in love at first cow.

This was the post-Vietnam War era, and Jim was just getting out of the army. He had a low draft number and decided to join up. He wanted to be a pilot, but he was disqualified because his eyesight was not twenty-twenty. Jim had a gift for languages and was sent to the Defense Language Institute in Monterey, California. He was then accepted into Intelligence school in Fort Huachuca, Arizona. Jim was scheduled to go to Germany from there, but his mission was canceled, and he was sent instead to Washington, DC, to conduct background checks, and meet me!

Jim had attended the University of Tulsa before joining the army and finished his degree at the University of Maryland. He wanted to become a dentist. Mom's death left me in limbo concerning my career as I could no longer save her and did not think I would do well in a profession that, in any way, included death as an outcome. This was the 70s, and women were becoming liberated from the idea of career exclusion. I thought dentistry would fit into my area of interest, and if I became a dentist, perhaps Jim would marry me. I wasn't fully liberated yet!

As I entered my second semester, I decided to look at dentistry as a career and made an appointment with my assigned advisor to check my chances. My grades were excellent, and my work experience was good, but there was one nagging question for me. All the dentists I knew had ten fingers, not seven. Could I even be accepted into dental school?

My advisor was an older man who smoked a big cigar while talking to me. I was intimidated. I asked him if he thought I could go to dental school with only seven fingers. He leaned back in his chair, puffing away on his cigar for a moment, then said with a smirk, "Of course not; no dental school will let you in with only seven fingers." Despite its arrogant delivery, his answer made sense to me. I was devastated. I would have to find another way to get Jim to marry me! I got up to leave, and just as I was about to close the door to the office, he added an addendum to his proclamation: "However, if you were a man, they might accept you."

What the heck! My devastation turned to rage. This man had no idea if I could go to dental school. He was willing to ruin my dream to save his ego. Instead of changing careers, I changed advisors.

Changing advisors was challenging in the days before student computer entry. I waited for several hours in line at the Advising Office before getting help. The clerks there were unhappy with a lowly freshman asking to change advisors, so they gave me Dr. Potter.

Dr. Potter was scary. She was my genetics professor and took pride in her high dropout rate. She told us the first day that half of us could not cut the mustard and would drop out soon. She was right! Dr. Potter seemed old; her hair was gray and tousled. She wore thin glasses low on her nose; her eyes would peer over them as she enlightened us on the latest advances in DNA sequencing. She looked like the inspiration for Marge Simpson's sisters on the long-running cartoon sitcom *The Simpsons*.

Dr. Potter smoked while she lectured. A frequent topic of conversation among her students was how she could hold a cigarette in her mouth and talk simultaneously. It was as if the cigarette was Velcroed to her lips! Not once during the entire semester did her cigarette fall.

When I was given Dr. Potter's name, my heart sank. But I was determined, and I found myself at her door in a few days. After a tentative knock, a surprisingly pleasant voice invited me in. Dr. Potter smiled and asked me to sit down. She listened intently to my story, and when I inquired if she thought I could be accepted to dental school, she said, "I don't know; let's find out!"

Dr. Potter then called the University of Maryland Dental School and made an appointment for me with Dr. Buchness, the Director of Restorative Dentistry. A week later, I was sitting in Dr. Buchness' office and asked him if I could be a dentist. He said, "Can you hold a mirror in your right hand?" I said, "Yes" and demonstrated my mirror-holding skills. He pronounced, "Well then, you can become a dentist, as only one hand goes to dental school, and the other holds the mirror." Who knew?

Dr. Potter encouraged me all through college and was elated that I was accepted into dental school a year early.

And oh, by the way, I got the guy!!

Jim and I were married my junior year, and we could attend dental school together. My plan worked out better than expected!

We both enjoyed dental school and made many lifelong friends. I had a small emotional crisis when we reached our junior year and were about to start seeing live patients. Although I could physically perform dental surgery and did very well in my classes, I was worried about what my patients would think about my lack of fingers. I was still very self-conscious about my hand and realized that I had to overcome my fears. I believed that a solution might be putting myself in a situation where I would have to hold up my hand in public. With that in mind, I became a member of the Baltimore Board of Officials and began officiating high school basketball games. I also officiated university intramural volleyball games. Both of these jobs were terrifying at first, but I got used to holding up both hands in front of lots of people. I also got used to people staring at my hand. I realized that the stares were typically not mean-spirited, just curious. After a while, I lost my fear of what patients would think of me. I find it amazing that in my thirty-plus years of practicing clinical dentistry, my finger shortfall was never an issue. My patients just wanted me to care about them and be technically proficient.

While in dental school, we both received National Health Service scholarships and became commissioned officers in the United States Public Health Service at graduation. We worked in Kankakee, Illinois, where our first child, Hillary, was born. We suffered a miscarriage two years later. I did a general practice residency, served as a clinical assistant professor at Loyola University Dental School, and discovered that I was pregnant again. We moved to Minnesota to be near Jim's family and bought a practice in Farmington, MN. Ashley was born in Farmington, followed by Eric three years later. We worked together in our dental practice, and Jim coached twenty-one seasons in various sports and activities for the kids. He became involved in community development. I became engaged in the community and served for fourteen years on the school board. I started a clinic for developmentally disabled adults in Faribault, Minnesota, and became active in the dental association, serving as the first woman president of the Minnesota Dental Association in 2000. The American Dental Association invited me to be a National Spokesperson, and I enjoyed that position for twenty-one years. Because we were practice owners and could adjust our schedules, we never missed a game or activity that our children were involved in. Life was good!

Things started to fall apart in 2007 when my brother Mike became the third member of our family to die of heart disease at fifty-six. Three months later, Jim was diagnosed with liver cancer. My desperate Internet searches gave him a 5 percent chance of living for five years or more, and all of the sources agreed. The doctors at Mayo Clinic said that his only chance was a liver transplant, and fortunately, because the disease was caught early, he was eligible. We lived close to Mayo, and on June 28, 2008, we got the call to get down to Rochester immediately. Jim's transplant was a success, and we can never thank the donor and his family enough, as well as the excellent doctors at The Mayo Clinic, for giving us this gift of life.

After the whirlwind of 2008, we thought that life would return to normal. Hillary graduated from law school and was working as a legal clerk, Ashley was attending her first year of law school at the University of St. Thomas Law School in Minneapolis, and Eric was studying engineering and in his first year of college at his dream school, Columbia University in New York.

We celebrated Christmas 2008 together at our newly built cabin and retirement home in the Chippewa National Forest. Eric wrote on his Facebook page that it was "The best Christmas ever." We spent New Year's Day on a sleigh ride and snow tubing excursion with Eric's friends.

Eric was delighted to learn he had made the dean's list at Columbia as an engineering major. This just topped off an incredible first semester. Eric had been elected to student government, had participated in theater with the students at Barnard College, and was accepted into the jazz program as a jazz pianist. Eric had inherited the best of my parents (and Jim's). He had the brains of my father (Eric was a National Merit Scholar) and the loving heart of my mother; he was also a brilliant musician and played three instruments. His favorite was piano.

We didn't realize that he might have also inherited the depression that seemed to have stalked every generation of my family.

Eric was in love with another young engineering student. Unfortunately, she was not equally in love with him, and two weeks into his second semester at Columbia, Eric's girlfriend broke up with him. This should have been a normal life challenge, but within forty-five minutes, Eric took his life, as my mother had done thirty-five years earlier. Our lives were shattered.

I don't remember much of those first weeks except I couldn't eat, I couldn't sleep, I couldn't think, and I felt for a long while that I couldn't continue. Jim and I thought we were in the depths of hell. We could hardly breathe. There seemed to be a big net strangling my heart and pulling me into the muck repeatedly. It was pulling Jim down too.

My identity was gone. On January 28, I was the mother of three in a family of five. A day later, I didn't know how to define myself. On the plane to New York for Eric's memorial, a woman asked me how many children I had. I panicked and froze; how many children did I have, or how many do I have? I avoided the question.

Columbia University was supportive. They even dedicated a permanent memorial, a shadbush, to Eric in front of the engineering building. The acting dean of engineering picked this tree because it reminded him of Eric. It was broad and giving. It had beautiful flowers in the spring, bore fruit in the summer, had colorful leaves in the fall, and the fruit fed the birds in the winter. Thank you, Columbia.

I felt for a long while that I would never get out of that pit of despair until, one day, I met another pit dweller. I was leaving the dental office one evening a few weeks after Eric died. Jim was standing with his cousin, whom I will call Carl (not his real name). Years ago, Carl had lost his teenage brother. The brother had been out drinking with friends and passed out. His friends drove him home and left him outside in his car. Unfortunately, it was a cold January night in Minnesota, and Carl's brother froze to death just steps away from his front door. Carl's parents never recovered, and Carl believes that he lost his parents emotionally the night his brother died. Frequently, the loss of a child can lead to the breakdown of a family; one heartache begets another. As I walked toward the cousins, Carl, with anger in his voice, shook his finger at me and said, "Don't you ever let your remaining children feel they are not enough!" At first, I was taken aback. I was a grieving mother; how dare he accuse me. But within a few seconds, I understood. Carl had given me a rare gift. I could look at his brokenness and see the future of my own family if I did not act. It was really up to me. Jim was just trying to stay alive after his liver transplant, and he was struggling physically and mentally.

I committed myself at that moment to redeeming my family. I was determined to use every ounce of energy to scratch and claw my way out of that pit. I had suffered bouts of depression before and knew I needed help. I sought treatment and am so glad I did. My doctor was a dear friend and found the proper medication for me. At one point, I tried to wean myself off the medication as I was embarrassed that I needed it. That was a mistake! After a couple of years, I realized that I would need to be treated for depression for the rest of my life, and I am so glad that treatment is available. For me, it works.

A year later, I lost my clinical career in one day. I had a lot of pain in my back, neck, and hands but was so distracted with Jim's medical issues that I assumed they were only due to my arthritis. When I finally visited the Mayo Clinic, the doctors told me that I had irreversible damage to the nerves in my neck that affected my drilling fingers and that my clinical career in dentistry was over. What the heck? Who could have predicted that it would be my good, fully fingered, hand that would take me out of dentistry?

I had little time to wallow over my fate as Jim's health began to decline. Jim's liver recovered from the transplant, but his heart was broken after Eric's death. A year after Eric died and at about the time my spine and hand problems were identified, Jim was diagnosed with several major heart issues. A few months later, he was undergoing quadruple bypass surgery and an aortic valve replacement at The Mayo Clinic in Rochester, MN. His recovery was bumpy, but in a few months, he was well enough to travel for a long-planned visit to Israel with our church. At the wailing wall, I wrote to God: "Please take care of Jim and the girls."

And God did!!

The next few years after Eric's death saw new joys and challenges. Hillary married Mike, Ashley married Joe, and our family rejoiced. God provided my girls with wonderful husbands who later became wonderful fathers. The grandchildren started coming with identical twin girls, Anna and Lily, followed by Eric, Heidi, Catherine, and Elizabeth (Lizzy). Our family grew to twelve. Jim and I reveled in grandparenthood.

We still missed Eric, our son, terribly, but we kept him alive in our hearts. Eric loved books, especially the classics. He liked to read them in Latin if he could. Whenever Eric heard of a library getting ready to dispose of books, he would go through them and rescue any classical literature he could find. A few months after Eric's death, my dear friend, Pam Pappas Stanoch, a board member for Books for Africa, suggested that we send a memorial library to honor Eric in Rwanda. There are now over sixty Eric Harms Memorial Libraries through Books for Africa in Rwanda. Rwanda became my healing place with the best grief counselors in the world. When it comes to building legacies, Rwanda is a rich source of material, as you will find throughout this book.

Jim's health continued to decline. For eight out of the next ten years, Jim suffered at least one death-defying illness, including losing over half his blood, several diabetic comas, bacterial endocarditis, septic shock, and a heart attack while intubated and in a drug-induced coma. At one point, his local doctors told us that his heart valve was failing, but because of his fragile state, nothing could be done.

Shortly afterward, we went to Kansas City for the birth of our fifth grandchild Catherine. Just as we were getting ready to go to the hospital, Jim found himself gasping for air. As Joe drove Ashely to the hospital to deliver Catherine, I drove Jim to the emergency room at the same hospital. Jim was stabilized and eventually placed in the cardiac unit, which happened to be on the same floor as the maternity ward. I ran back and forth from Jim's room to Ashley's room. I was able to see my beautiful granddaughter Catherine make her perfectly timed debut into the world and then wheel Jim and his oxygen tank down the hall to the maternity ward so that he could join the newly enlarged family. A few days later, Jim was transferred to the regional heart hospital, and the doctors at St. Luke's gave Jim a new trans aortic valve replacement (TAVR) and four more years of life. During those years, Jim got to meet one more grandchild, Lizzy, and have four more years of adventures with the other five.

Jim suffered more decline, then he started falling, broke his shoulder, and a few months later, he decided he was done with hospitals. He wanted to enter hospice at home. Jim did not want to ever be intubated again or die in a hospital. On August 7, 2020 (what would have been our son Eric's thirty-first birthday), Jim stopped breathing, and his heart stopped beating. I was just getting him out of the tub. I panicked, and although he was DNR (do not resuscitate), I attempted rescue breathing. It didn't work. Even though Jim was in hospice, I was not ready for him to die. I called the hospice nurses to tell them he was gone and sent a cryptic text to my dear friend Darlene and then I called Hillary to tell her of the news. We cried on the phone for at least ten minutes. But wait! Twenty minutes after his last breath, while I was on the phone with Hillary, and as the hospice nurse approached our condo door, Jim suddenly took one big deep breath, just like in the movies, and started breathing normally again. I dropped the phone and shouted, "He's alive!" and he was! The nurse jumped into action and summoned rescuers to get him into bed. He was breathing but not conscious. A few minutes later, Jim woke up right on cue!

He was extremely weak, and his body no longer worked, but his brain was intact. Amazing! He asked why he was in bed because the last thing he remembered was in the bathtub. I have to admit I was hoping for a near-death vision of God and Eric welcoming him home to heaven. Still, I realized that there would be no way that Jim would return from a reunion with his Savior and his son in heaven to his terribly weakened body back on Earth. I was so glad to have Jim back, but I also realized he did not have much time. I called his brothers and sisters and nieces and nephews and told them of Jim's condition, and we all had the most fantastic day together. The incredible thing was that not only was Ashley in town, but so was our niece, Laura, who was a nurse practitioner at Presbyterian Hospitals in New York. (This was in 2020, and much of the country was still limited in travel.) Laura was on a rare break visiting her sister Anna (also a nurse). Anna and Laura had spent a lot of time at our home when they were kids, and it meant so much to Jim that they were there. Our nephew, Joel, and his family also came to the vigil. Joel and Jim were not only close, but they were also very much alike!

Jim had his brothers and sisters, nieces and nephews, and daughters and sons-in-law surrounding him for the rest of the day. He got to have all the Diet Pepsi and ice cream he wanted. Anna and Laura propped him up on pillows and ensured he was comfortable. A brother who had not talked to Jim for several years brought old home movies. It was a beautiful reconciliation.

The out-of-staters spoke to him on Zoom, and amazingly, he was alert and happy the entire day. He passed away very peacefully early the next morning. We were so grateful for that miraculous gift of twenty-one hours.

I am now the oldest member of my immediate family, meaning I should be the next to go! I want to be the next to go. I want to follow the natural order. Losing a parent or grandparent is an expected part of life. Losing a child is not. With that in mind, I want to ensure that my survivors have everything they need to thrive when I am gone. I hope to pass on some of the wisdom that I've learned from my life experiences to help them with theirs. I want to leave them with all of my affairs in order and emotionally prepared for the time when I am gone.

Death is the great equalizer! The most learned man from the greatest institution has the same right to his belief about death as the poorest person in the most distant land on earth. In the US, according to the 2014 Pew Research Center Religious Landscape Study[1], only 7 percent of the population reported being agnostic or atheist. The vast majority of Americans and, indeed, the world believe in a higher power. That faith significantly shapes our focus on what we believe happens after death. For those who believe in an afterlife, it just makes sense to help the people we leave behind in the best shape possible. For those who believe that their existence is limited to the short time spent alive on Earth, it would seem to make even more sense to be concerned about the fate of their loved ones who continue on. Throughout this book, I will refer to that higher power as God. Because I am a Christian, Jesus is God too. For this book to be authentic, I need to speak from my heart and with the language of my heart. For those who speak a different faith language,

---

[1] https://www.pewresearch.org/religion/religious-landscape-study/.

please make the appropriate translations in your heart. I hope that this book can be interpreted by all with an open mind and willing heart and be applied to your life in a way that fits you. Our denial of death is a logical defense mechanism in a society that has extended life expectancies and focuses on wellness. But since no one in the history of humanity has yet escaped death, I think it is time to change the narrative. Let's show our survivors how much we love them by ensuring our affairs are in order. Even more important, let's focus on leaving them an amazing legacy of love, trust, peace, education, generosity, compassion, or whatever values are important to us. Spend time together now, laugh together now, play together now, and be there in times of crisis and grief.

This book is written to help you build a legacy while you are living, to help you die well when the time comes, and then to help you leave a loving remembrance to your survivors. Hopefully, you have already made a start, but if you haven't, let's start now!

Resources:

The Necessity of Legacy: Why Your Story Is Needed and How to Make It Last by Jeremy Brown.

Legacy: A Step by Step Guide to Writing Personal History by Linda Spence.

https://www.youtube.com/watch?v=DMHMOQ_054U 4 Stages of Retirement.

https://youtu.be/rmuTvYo2JkA Rethink Retirement.

https://www.youtube.com/watch?v=sL3Ntcb50wA. Fix the Damn Roof! By John Turnipseed at TEDxTC

https://www.fivestonemedia.com/the-turnipseed-trilogy/

https://www.youtube.com/watch?v=LteZuADO780

The Legacy of Love

*Love is made up of three unconditional
properties in equal measure:
Acceptance
Understanding
Appreciation
Remove any one of these three, and the triangle falls apart.
Which, by the way, is something highly inadvisable. Think
about it-do you really want to live in a world with two
dimensions? So, for the love of a triangle, please keep love whole.*
—Vera Nazarian

Love is the greatest feeling on Earth. It affects everything we do. It is sometimes defined as having two parts, an interest or pleasure in something and an attachment. It requires thinking beyond oneself and putting the needs of others before yourself. There are many types of love, but the ones that most of us are familiar with are passionate love, love of family and friends, love of a parent for a child, and Agape love, which is the unconditional love of mankind (think Mother Teresa).

Love and kindness go hand in hand. I was blessed with love for the first part of my life with my mom and for forty-four years of my adult life with my husband Jim. Having someone love you gives you a secure base to grow and expand. But how do we teach love to future generations? We show love in everything we do!

One of my favorite words is a strange one: eudaimonia. Eudaimonia goes beyond happiness and is considered the highest human good. It is a feeling that transcends a lifetime. According to *Positive Psychology*, "the most common elements in definitions of eudaimonia are growth, authenticity, meaning, and excellence. Together, these concepts provide a reasonable idea of what most researchers mean by eudaimonia."[2]

I think most of us strive throughout our lives to achieve eudaimonia. According to Ethics.org, the closest word in English is flourishing or living our lives well. Who doesn't want to flourish? According to Ethics.org, "the eudaimon life is one dedicated to developing the excellences of being human. For Aristotle, this meant practicing virtues like courage, wisdom, good humor, moderation, kindness, and more."[3]

Mom was a master of expressing love. Not only did she tell us she loved us, but she was also physically affectionate. She would pull out the mattresses from the bedroom every weekend, and we would "camp out" in front of the fireplace. Then she would make fudge, and we would listen to records and dance, play games and tell stories. At Christmas, Santa would always show up at the door with gifts. We were mesmerized. On my last Christmas with Mom, I got a pair of puppy dog pajamas with a flap in the back. I wore those pajamas until the elastic wore out. For my fifth birthday, she played a song sung by Danny Kaye entitled "I Am Five." I loved that song and played it repeatedly until the record broke. I play it now, on my phone, for all of my grandchildren when they turn five. It is a gift from their great-grandmother.

One night for my birthday, Mom took me to a special restaurant with a big grand piano. After dinner, Mom brought me up

---

[2] https://positivepsychology.com/eudaimonia/.

[3] https://ethics.org.au/ethics-explainer-eudaimonia/.

to the piano, and the pianist sang a song "Kim" to me in front of the entire restaurant. I had never felt so special.

Mom also modeled to me the value of unconditional love. She put her children first; she had my back. She predicted times when I would have difficulty and prepared me. On my first day of school, Mom was worried that the other kids might make fun of my unusual hand. She told me that God had a special purpose for me and that He didn't make mistakes and that the other kids might not understand this, and that people naturally criticize things they don't understand. She had a long talk with my first-grade teacher, Sister Mary Anne before I started. Sister repeated the "You are special" philosophy to me when the kids teased. On the first day of school, when no other child would hold my hand as we walked in procession from the playground to the classroom, my teacher suggested that I hold the hand of my guardian angel. Unfortunately, it was my guardian angel's first day of class too. He led me into the wrong classroom. I stood paralyzed, arm still out in holding hands formation, speechless and staring at an unfamiliar class and teacher. It took a few minutes, but the Sisters eventually worked things out, and I was placed back into the hands of the right teacher. When I get to heaven, I plan to have a laugh with my guardian angel over that one!

One of the most important legacies we can leave is to help those we love to live a good life. How do we do that? We need to express and model love, gratitude, and joy. My mom, as fractured as she was, taught me these qualities in only six years. I could never understand how unconditional love received for such a short time and at such a young age would not be counteracted by many years of abuse and neglect suffered later.

Several years ago, I found the answer! I was working with 5 Stone Media to assist them with a video project designed to help church leaders minister to those who were struggling with mental illness. My incredible friend, Terri Hands, formed a group of mental health professionals (and one dentist) to provide ideas for this project. We called ourselves "The Trauma Tribe." It was there I met Melinda Cathey, M.A. Melinda is a remarkable therapist who worked in orphanages in Russia and Ukraine and explained the concept of attachment theory to me. We were working together to help 5 Stone Media develop a program for church groups to deal with grief, loss, and mental illness. Just as I was getting ready to welcome our fourth grandchild into the world, Melinda explained to me that to help our children become happy, loving, thankful, and responsible adults, we must work hard to attach to them when they are young.

According to Wikipedia, "Attachment theory is a psychological, evolutionary, and ethnological theory concerning relationships between humans. The most important tenet is that young children need to develop a relationship with at least one primary caregiver for normal social and emotional development. The theory was formulated by psychiatrist and psychoanalyst John Bowlby."[4]

What does this mean? It means we must intentionally parent our children and focus clearly on the important people in our lives when they are young. When Melinda explained this to me, especially citing the research that found that neglected kids (such as those Melinda worked with in Eastern European orphanages) had a harder time adjusting to life than abused kids, I was floored. How does that happen? Small children need mental stimulation and emotional nurturing in addition to their physical needs. If they don't get it, their brain changes, making them incapable of developing the emotional attachments we need to survive well as humans.

---

[4] https://en.wikipedia.org/wiki/Attachment_theory.

I believe that my ability to flourish and thrive as an adult despite the losses I suffered has much to do with my mother. For six years (except for the train track incident described in chapter one), she loved me, paid attention to me, made me feel important, taught me gratitude, and gave me my faith. Mom ensured I felt valuable. These characteristics sustained me even when she was not around. Those early years in my life with my mom were crucial to my success as an adult.

After meeting Melinda, I vowed always to stay attuned to my grandchildren. When with them, I focus on them and their needs, not mine. I put away social media. And although I may temporarily fall behind in my emails, I know our personal interactions enrich my life and theirs.

According to Melinda in an article for 5 Stone Media:

"When a baby is born, it has needs it cannot meet; physical needs such as being fed, clothed, and diapers being changed. It also has emotional needs for comfort, touch, talking, etc. To get its needs met, the only power this helpless, vulnerable baby has is to cry. God's design is that a caretaker will meet those needs in a quick, adequate, predictable, and warm or nurturing way. When a caretaker does this, they give experiential messages of love and care to the baby:

I see you
I hear you
I will be here for you; you are not alone
I will comfort you
I will protect you
I will meet your needs
I will delight in you
When a baby experiences this cycle of having needs and being cared for over and over and over again in

the first three years of life, he/she incorporates these
messages deep inside their soul. They come to believe:
I am pretty special
I can get my needs met; I have some power
I am valued, loved, I belong to someone
The world is safe and predictable
People are good and kind and trustworthy
When these are your narratives, you are at peace. You are open
to trusting and connecting with others. You will go to others for
comfort. Your body will be able to relax. This is actually reflected
in your muscles, heart rate, digestion, etc. Your brain will secrete
balancing and pleasurable neurotransmitters like dopamine
and serotonin. And your brain is freed up to develop more
connections in the higher-functioning part of your brain, the
cortex. This is the part of your brain you use to learn, to develop
empathy, to have self-control, to reflect, and to attach to others.[5]

Love and kindness go hand in hand, although sometimes love is "tough" when lessons need to be learned. I am in that stage in life where I am not responsible for the development and upbringing of anyone but myself. This gives me the freedom to go into "Granny Mode." Every problem can be solved with a hug and a cookie. Okay, well, maybe it is not quite that simple, and my grandchildren are young and will soon face adult problems that are more complex, but I am enjoying this moment in time.

Kindness can be simple. Every birthday, anniversary, and holiday, for over thirty years, Jim and I received a card from an amazing couple, Paul and Kathy Rieke. Theirs is not an official ministry, but a personal mission of encouragement provided to many people. When I receive a Rieke greeting, I feel less

---

[5] https://lifesupportresources.org/perfect-love-casts-out-fear/.

isolated. I know someone has been thinking about me, that they took the time to pick out a card, write a message, and then put it in the mail. A written correspondence feels more personal than an email message as I can touch it, it has depth, and I feel emotionally attached to the sender. Over the years, Jim and I have been the beneficiaries of over one hundred written affirmations from Paul and Kathy. Hopefully, I passed that positivity on to others. The Reike card ministry just keeps on giving!

As we age, the difficulties in life may seem so big they fracture relationships, and the love (although still present) gets lost. One of the problems that older adults with broken relationships face is that they would like their families to be there for them as they decline but don't know how to begin to repair the relationship. Children who feel that their parents were not available to them while growing up may be resentful if they believe that their parents expect to return to their lives and be taken care of by them as they age. Grief after the loss of a parent is hard enough, but when a broken relationship is involved, it is typically even more complicated. In this situation, both parties lose.

Acceptance is a big part of love. If we work to accept family members who we may not agree with, we can keep that relationship going for a lifetime. On the other hand, it is important to remember that we need to set boundaries. Lysa Terkeurst, in her book, *Good Boundaries and Good-byes,* states, "We must require from people the responsibility necessary to grant the amount of access we allow them to have in our lives." In other words, you can love people without letting them walk all over you! When you set healthy boundaries, you can forgive, love, and even reconcile without putting your emotional health in danger.

Recently, while attending a conference, I got to know an extraordinary young woman, Dr. Jessica Metcalfe. Jessica has recently published a book, *Speak Kindly, You're Listening,* in which she says, "Have you ever thought of how you speak to yourself; the words you choose? The tone of voice? The pitch or volume? Just as you use different voices when speaking to a child, parent, or lover, have you noticed that you use a different voice when you speak to yourself?" Jessica focuses this book on helping people treat themselves the same way they treat the other people they love. I have to admit that in my younger days, I spent a lot of time badgering myself with shame and guilt in a way I would never speak to my friends or family. It wasn't until I reached my fifties that I finally accepted myself with all of my imperfections. Why did I cause myself so much unnecessary misery? We all go through periods of awkwardness and uncertainty, but fifty years? I hope that I can help my children and grandchildren accept themselves for who they are and accept others in the same way. It is hard to love others when we don't love ourselves. I spoke to Jessica recently, and she said, "We give permission and compassion for everyone around us, but not ourselves. If your friend is having a bad day and she is suffering from disappointment, guilt, or shame, wouldn't you do your best to uplift her and help her feel better? Even though we can be that voice for someone else, if we are put into that exact same situation, our inner critic can be louder, meaner, and ruder to ourselves." Jessica, where were you when I was twenty? This information could have saved me from thirty years of accepting the voice of my rude inner critic.

Kurt Vonnegut wrote, "A purpose of human life, no matter who is controlling it, is to love whoever is around to be loved." I love that quote, and it is so true.

Love and happiness go hand in hand. According to an eighty-five-year Harvard Health Study (we will go more into depth in this in the Legacy of Friendship chapter), happiness can be achieved in many ways. The study found that you can work on happiness by staying connected to friends and family. You can also volunteer and help others, perform and plan acts of kindness, pick hobbies and activities that make you happy, and delegate tasks to buy more time. Investing in experiences can also make you happier, as can surrounding yourself with happy people. The researchers also found that you can work towards more happiness by creating green space, trying new things, creating a gratitude journal, and making fewer decisions.[6] I believe that the most important legacy we can leave is love. It transcends all age groups and cultures. It "makes the world go round" (W.S. Gilbert). Recently, while working with widows at the Red Rocks Cultural Center in Rwanda, I was trying to explain the concept of the importance of legacy. This was a group of very poor older women who were born before the education language in Rwanda was changed to English. Unfortunately, I was not fluent in the Rwandan native language of Kinyarwandan, and we needed an interpreter. I was not making much headway in my description of leaving a legacy. The women felt that they had no ability to leave a legacy as they had nothing to give. Fortunately, there was one thing we did share, we were all of the same faith. Through the understanding of our faith, I asked them, "Who left the greatest legacy of all time?" Their answer was Jesus. "What legacy did He leave?" Their answer was love. Suddenly every face lit up. These remarkable women, some of whom became widows and lost their entire families during the 1994 Genocide, understood that no matter how poor they were, they all had the capacity to leave the greatest legacy ever, love.

How much love can you leave to the people in your life?

---

[6] https://www.health.harvard.edu/mind-and-mood/health-and-happiness-go-hand-in-hand.

Resources:

The Good Life: Lessons from the World's Longest Study of Happiness
by Robert M.D. and Marc Schulz PhD, Simon and Schuster.

5 Stone Media: https://www.fivestonemedia.com.

Speak Kindly, You're Listening by Dr. Jessica Metcalfe.

Good Boundaries and Good-byes by Lysa Terkeurst.

https://www.psychologytoday.com/us/blog/anger-in-the-age
-entitlement/201301/love-and-values.

https://www.redrocksrwanda.com.

The Legacy of Hard Work

*A dream does not become reality through magic; it
takes sweat, determination, and hard work.*
—Colin Powell

We can learn to work hard in many ways. Some of us learn
through deprivation, some through inspiration. Our motivations can be intrinsic (we love what we do) or extrinsic (external rewards for hard work such as a paycheck). Most of us
would like to live up to Mark Twain's quote, "Find a job you
like, and you will never have to work a day in your life." The
reality, however, is that many of the things we love doing do
not correlate with a living wage. Most of us must actually work
for a living in a field that, although we may enjoy most of the
time, has its stressors. Some of us find ourselves in a working
environment we don't like at all.

There are very special people out there, however, who seem
to thrive and have joy and are motivated and cheerful no matter
what they are doing. What's their secret?

One of the important ingredients to enjoying hard work is the
cultivation of gratitude no matter your circumstances. Another
is focusing on developing healthy relationships at work. Taking
time to laugh, helping a coworker, getting enough sleep, exer-
cising, and eating healthier can go a long way to making you
happier at work.

Years ago, when porters were more available to check in your luggage curbside at the airport, I would always search for a specific Northwest Airlines porter/agent. No matter what the weather (Minneapolis can get *very* cold), no matter how many people were standing in line, he was smiling and jovial. He was efficient too. He always had the longest line. (I suspect others were porter groupies like me.) Our line seemed to move much faster than the other lines. I am not sure how much of the "faster" perception was attributed to his actual, efficient delivery of service or that when someone is laughing and smiling and essentially entertaining you, the wait seems shorter. He was an older gentleman, and eventually, he was no longer there to greet us before our flight. I suspect he retired. Flying was never the same.

My husband Jim, as the twelfth of fourteen children raised on a farm, learned the value of hard work early in life. Jim's dad, Sam, was a hardworking farmer who emigrated with his family from Germany to escape the tumultuous times leading up to World War I. He eventually became a successful farmer and, because he could speak German, hosted German prisoners of war who worked on his farm during World War II. Jim's mom, Inez, got up early in the morning, baked bread, prepared the meals, watched after the children, and, when needed, got out on the tractor to help with farm chores. She delivered her babies at home and the next day was up, helping clean the house for company. Before we got married, I made Jim swear never to compare me to his mother. She was a Superwoman. They don't make women like that anymore! Still, Inez would tell you she led a good life, and hard work was part of the good.

When Jim was around ten years old, his father started to decline due to back pain, then a stroke, then dementia. Jim remembers his father, as weak as he was, trying to help grade potatoes in the warehouse. He also remembers his mother (close to sixty at this time) hauling around fifty-pound potato sacks. Inez had amazing biceps. One picture, taken when Inez was close to seventy, shows her with her sons in their favorite muscle-flexing pose. Inez's biceps, placed side by side, were bigger than her frame, and all the muscle bulging was on the top of her arm. Besides passing on her legacy of hard work, she also passed on a legacy of love and kindness. Later in her life, after she had a stroke, she told Eric that she wanted to stay alive until he, her youngest grandchild, graduated from high school. Inez measured her lifespan in terms of her grandchildren. Unfortunately, she didn't make it to Eric's graduation and died at ninety-one, a beloved matriarch with well over one hundred hard-working descendants.

Jim's youngest sister, Lois, traces her remarkable work ethic back to the onion fields of her youth, where she learned to weed alongside her thirteen brothers and sisters. She wrote a short story about her experiences; here is an excerpt:

"Line up and get ready to weed!" my sister Georgia spoke loudly. "Lois needs my help this morning, so do your three rows, and I'll start Lois with one row."

I was only five years old, and my teammates were thirteen brothers and sisters. "Are there any questions? Make sure you pull the weeds from the roots and don't forget the thistles, or otherwise, you'll have to come back and do it over again. Do it right the first time. Keep your eyes on the finish line. Let's get started. Get on your mark, get set, go!" commanded Georgia, our straw boss.

The race began.

In the hot summer sun, we needed to weed twenty acres of onions, which is equivalent to ten city blocks. The team, my family, made a game of it, like playing tree tag or trench. The age of my family was five to thirteen years old. My older brothers were helping Dad cultivate. We were children doing an important job for the family. This game of weeding onions had more instructions and was hard work. The job was easier if we played some games. We dressed in cotton pants, long-sleeve white shirts, with a swimming suit underneath, so we could go swimming at the sand pit, after weeding.

Dad had a vegetable farm of 110 acres of potatoes, acres of onions and other vegetables, and fruit. We weeded the fields in summer, harvested in fall, and graded/bagged potatoes along with the onions into the winter. Mom was home doing wash in her Maytag wringer washing machine, hanging clothes on the clothesline, making meals for sixteen members of the family. Mom was a very hard worker. The year was 1956.

"I know this is scary, looking at this big field, but I'm going to teach you to weed, so you will learn to weed as fast as your brothers and sisters, okay?" "Will you help me? I asked. "I can't do this," I said with a whimper. "I'll stay by you," Georgia reassured me. "Let's pull weeds."

"Row, row, row your boat gently down the stream. Merrily, merrily, merrily, merrily, life is but a dream." I heard someone sing. Soon everyone was singing. The round had started. I heard laughter. I joined in while pulling the weeds. All of us knew how to sing. We sang patriotic songs, Christian songs, nursery rhymes, all sorts of songs to make us happy.

This isn't so bad, I thought. We sang for a half hour or so. Georgia showed me how to pull the weeds, pull thistles without getting pricked, how to keep my feet cool by putting them deep in the dirt, and how to get fast at pulling weeds and keep going. My sister taught me well. Even if we could not see the end of the row, we needed to finish the row before we could take a break. We heard some hollering ahead of us.

"Quit throwing dirtballs at me!" I heard Jim holler (seven years old). "Well then, get up and start working! You missed some thistles back there!" my brother Tom shouted (nine years old). Jim threw some dirtballs back at Tom.

Georgia rushed over to the boys before the squabble got out of hand "Hey, you guys, no more dirtballs now. We won't have any fighting out here. We need to get the work done." She had spoken with authority. The boys calmed down. We all went back to work.

Finally, I could see my family get done with the rows, which were the length of three city blocks. The rule was—you did not take a break until you helped the ones who were behind with their rows.

We finished the race together. No exceptions. I needed help to finish. Finally, we were done. We celebrated by taking a break, only to start again.

Fortunately, we no longer live in a world (at least in the US) where five-year-olds are required to work. But when faced with that necessity on a family farm years ago, the Harms family discovered that the secret to success was making even the most menial work fun!

A few years ago, I met a remarkable young woman who had a hard work legacy successfully passed down to her from her father, mother, and grandfather, and who was now modeling that behavior to inspire others. Minal Sampat is a bestselling author, nationally known speaker, and marketing strategist who attributes much of her success to her supportive family and the example they showed to her.

In a Facebook post, Minal recently shared with us a glimpse into the special familial magic she shared.

"When I was a little girl in India," she writes, "we lived in a house with a beautiful hand-carved wooden porch swing. Everyone loved the swing and took turns sitting on it to enjoy the sunshine, breeze, and passing of the day.

"Every day, my uncle (who was a dentist) and I would sit on the swing, and he would tell me stories. Stories about his childhood, travels, happenings in the dental office, music, and life experiences.

"This was my favorite part of my day: to learn about the past, live in the present, and dream about the future."

From this description of her childhood and knowing of her success, you might assume that Minal came from a long background of at least moderate wealth and privilege. You would be wrong! Minal's hard work hero was her homeless, widowed great-grandmother and her son, Minal's grandfather, Kastur Sampat.

Minal is a vibrant and energetic person, and when she starts talking about her family, her face lights up even more. She explains, "Grandad Sampat came from nothing. His father passed away when he was a toddler, and his siblings did not make it to adulthood. Grandad Sampat spent his childhood going from town to town with his widowed mother to sell clothing. This was in a time that was not kind to a single, widowed, working woman. As a teenager, he decided that there had to be a better life. Since there was no money for formal education, he took it upon himself to self-educate. He even ranked number one in the state boards without having the luxury of being taught in a regular classroom setting."

"As he grew into an adult, his character and work ethic became so infectious that a woman from a prosperous house decided to marry him despite his lack of fortune. Together, they built a home and a family. Education and integrity became the pillars of the Sampat household. How lucky am I to know that I can reach out to any of my uncles, aunts, and cousins, and without hesitation, they will be there for me."

"I am where I am today because one man had the courage and tenacity to change his life, and one woman decided to love without prejudice."

Minal's grandparents eventually went on to have ten children, and they ensured that all of them learned the value of hard work by working in the family clothing business. They also made sure that every child received a good education and contributed to the community. Kastur Sampat transformed his family from homeless and impoverished to successful and philanthropic in one generation, and if Minal is the example from the next generation, the metamorphosis continues!

Minal's story is a fabulous example of multiple family members building each generation up with the melding of several legacies together, such as love, education, hard work, and resilience. Wow!

My friend and long-time dental colleague, Teresa Fong Sit, shared with me the incredible story of her grandfather Chie "Chee" Fong. Chee was born in China and came to the US in 1918 when he was ten years old. Before boarding the ship, he drank a special bowl of soup that sealed his engagement to a young girl he had never met, who would become Teresa's grandmother, Ming.

After spending a month in a detention center, in Seattle, WA, Chee joined his father, who had left his mother and their two children in China, to pursue the extended family's dream of finding gold in California. Chee's father was from a poor family, and because he had a bad temper, he was considered an expendable son. Therefore, he was the one chosen by his family to seek their fortune of gold in California so that the family could purchase more farmland in China. What the family didn't know is that California had laws that forbade Chinese immigrants from panning for gold, and Chee's father found himself alone in a foreign land with no means of support for himself and certainly no easy way to bring wealth to his family. He did, however, have some family in Arkansas, where the laws allowed the Chinese to own farmland if they owned a business. Chee's father moved to Round Pond, Arkansas, worked very hard, and eventually owned both.

As soon as he was settled, he sent for his ten-year-old son, Chee. Chee quickly learned English and to read and write. Education was important. Four years later, Chee's father became ill and returned to China. He left his fourteen-year-old son a grocery store, a shotgun, and $200. "At fourteen," Chee would frequently tell his family, "I became a man."

Chee's business grew nicely in the next four years. At eighteen, he was secure enough to go back to China to marry Ming. Shortly afterward, he left Ming and his family behind when he came back to the US to take care of his business. Chee traveled back to China every year for visits, which were apparently productive because, in a few short years, Chee and Ming had three children.

After the depression was over Chee brought his family back to the US with him. In the 1930s, they moved to Hughes, Arkansas, to open Fong's Department Store. As in many family businesses, all of the children eventually worked for the store; the working age started after the completion of second grade. Hard work was expected from the children and grandchildren, but it was also made to be fun. "Every Thursday," Teresa explains, "Grandfather would fish in the morning, take a nap, and then spend the afternoon in the shoe department, sitting with us and telling stories about growing up in China, his journey to the US, and what happened afterward." One of the frequent questions Chee was asked was, "How could you marry someone sight unseen?" His answer was that, in those days, it was believed that two reasonable people should be able to get along. He also told his grandchildren that at eighty years old, "My only job in life is to make this woman [his wife] happy." Perhaps that is why Ming and Chee stayed happily married for seventy-eight years! Teresa remembers her grandfather lovingly as "a simple man, very content, a hard worker with high moral standards, and an unshakable faith in God." He passed these standards on to his children and grandchildren.

Another legacy Chee passed down to his descendants was to freely talk about his death. He told his grandchildren, "When I die, I don't want anyone to cry. You can be sad, but you don't have to cry. I have lived an extraordinary life; I have been everywhere I wanted to go. I can die knowing that I have done everything I wanted to do. I am not afraid of death. At my funeral, I want Psalm 23 recited and 'When the Saints Come Marching In' and 'My Old Kentucky Home' sung." He was able to talk to his family about death without any fear or sadness. Chie "Chee" Fong was a man ahead of his time.

Recently I attended the funeral of our long-time family physician and friend Dr. Souheil Ailabouni. Souheil was Palestinian and from the village of Ailaboun. He fled the tribulation in his home country and came to America with $300 and the dream of becoming a physician. Through hard work, determination, and the support of his American wife Melli (they met at college in Nebraska) his dream was fulfilled. The couple eventually bought a solo medical practice in Farmington and Souheil "practiced modern medicine the old-fashioned way". My family was blessed and spoiled by Dr. Ailabouni's care. As medicine changed and became more impersonal, Souheil's practice (with Melli at the reception desk) remained family-oriented and personal. His was the last solo medical practice in our area. It was his extremely early diagnosis of liver cancer in my husband, Jim, that made it possible for Jim to get a liver transplant and gave our family 13 bonus years of having Jim in our lives. Without Souheil, it would be unlikely that our grandchildren would have been able to meet the PopPop who loved them so much. Dr. Ailabouni left a lasting legacy to the benefit of our family and the thousands of other lives he touched in our small town.

Hard work, determination, setting goals and serving others builds character and can increase your happiness in life. I feel so blessed to have married a man who received the legacy of hard work appreciation from his family. The families that my daughters married into also valued hard work. What can you do to pass this legacy on to your survivors?

Resources:
Do Hard Things: A Teenage Rebellion Against Low Expectations by Alex and Brett Harris.
The Seven Habits of Highly Effective People by Steven Covey.
The Seven Habits of Highly Effective Teens by Steven Covey.

The Legacy of Resilience

Pressure, challenges, they are all an opportunity for me to rise.

—*Kobe Bryant*

Wouldn't it be great if life was easy, if we could get through it without any sorrow or pain or death or disappointment? But the reality is that life is not easy: life is hard. The older you get, the more loss you suffer. Think about it, either you die young, or you watch the people you love die around you. But interestingly, many studies show that older people (Perennials), despite their decaying bodies, declining memories, and frequent attendance at funerals, are one of the happiest demographic groups around. How can this be? Happy seniors have discovered the power of resilience!

According to the American Psychological Association, "Resilience is the process and outcome of successfully adapting to difficult or challenging life experiences, especially through mental, emotional, and behavioral flexibility, and adjustment to external and internal demands."

We are all different in how we cope with loss, rejection, financial insecurity, the death of a loved one, and other hardships we face. Why can some people seem to "bounce back" after a loss while others are stuck in despair mode for years or even the rest of their lives? How do we transition from suffering to happiness, pessimism to optimism, bemoaning the past to embracing the present?

World Psychiatry tells us that "responses to trauma and significant stressors are determined by multiple dynamics, interacting individual-level systems (e.g., genetic, epigenetic, developmental, neurobiological), which are embedded in larger social systems (e.g., family, cultural, economic, and political systems)."[7]

In real people's words, each of us responds to stress in a unique fashion based on our history. Some of us bend; some of us break. The good news is that resilience can be built over time through experience and personal growth, increasing our ability to accept change, maintaining a hopeful outlook, improving our physical health, and improving our connections with others. Even those currently weak in managing emotional pain can strengthen their abilities to adapt to life's ever-changing realities. We can train our brains to overcome life's pain through mindfulness, gratefulness for what we have, and a positive attitude. I believe older people are more resilient because they have had more experience dealing with emotional pain.

My dear friend, Naomi Rhode, who is currently in her mid-eighties, introduced the Welcoming Prayer to me. The Welcoming Prayer is a great resilience builder. I have used this prayer many times to help me remember that I am not in control and to embrace the life I am living now.

The Welcoming Prayer (by Father Thomas Keating)
Welcome, welcome, welcome.
*I welcome everything that comes to me today because I
know it's for my healing. I welcome all thoughts, feelings,
emotions, persons, situations, and conditions.*
I let go of my desire for power and control.
I let go of my desire for affection, esteem, approval, and pleasure.

---

[7] https://www.ncbi.nlm.nih.gov/pmc/articles/PMC4780285/.

I let go of my desire for survival and security.
I let go of my desire to change any situation,
condition, person or myself.
I open to the love and presence of God
and God's action within. Amen.

For me, this prayer is a valuable aid for facing small trauma and for healing, not necessarily during a major traumatic event. I would not recommend sending this prayer to someone the day after their spouse died, for example. We are human, and suffering is painful. We should not trivialize it. Once the traumatic event is over and the initial phases of grief have been worked through, The Welcoming Prayer allows us to focus on facing our future with resilience, optimism, and courage.

Keeping things in perspective is one of the most important qualities we can model for our children. And if we model it well enough, we can pass on our legacy of resilience through our story. The story that inspired me to seek resilience for over forty years was that of Etta Hauptman.

In dental school, I was seated alphabetically with the *G*s and *H*s. My lab partner was Ron Hauptman.

At some point during our freshman year, Ron told me about his aunt and uncle, Etta and Ignatz Hauptman, and their daughter, Carol. Their horrific story of survival through the Holocaust was so profound it stayed with me for over forty years and helped me to understand the importance of resilience. After Eric's death, I thought of Etta often and vowed to do everything I could to model her example to my husband and surviving children.

When I decided to write this book, I felt it important to include their story. I called Ron and asked him to repeat the narrative to ensure I got the facts right. He said, "Why don't you talk to Carol, she is in Switzerland right now, and she travels a lot, but I will ask her if she will agree to an interview."

A few weeks later, I was on a Zoom call with the remarkable woman whose story had stayed with me and influenced my life for over forty years.

Trigger Warning: Crimes against humanity, including children.

Carol's family was Jewish and from Eastern Europe. The borders changed frequently in Eastern Europe; Carol was born in Boryslav, Ukraine, but by the time the Nazis came, it had become Boryslav, Poland. Her father, Ignatz, had lived in Vienna and spoke excellent German, which ultimately helped the family survive the war. At first, the family lived outside the Jewish Ghetto because Ignatz served as an interpreter. They had to wear a yellow Star of David to identify as Jewish. As a result of Ignatz's job as an interpreter, he learned of the pogroms which the Nazis scheduled every few weeks. (According to the Oxford Dictionary, a pogrom is "an organized massacre of a particular ethnic group, in particular that of Jewish people in Russia or eastern Europe in the late nineteenth and early twentieth centuries.")

During this time, Carol remembers, "My mother had a dream, and in this dream, my grandfather, who had died, appeared to her. He told her to wake up and run, run with the baby, just run. And she woke up from this dream and woke up my father and told him of the dream. And my father said, 'Do it!' Grab the baby and run.' They went to the window and could already hear the police coming and the Nazi soldiers marching. The Jews had to wear a yellow armband, and I was about eighteen months old. My mother just took off our yellow armbands and walked down the street, and they let her go. We hid for several days, and then my father realized we couldn't live there anymore. The only place we could possibly survive was in the ghetto itself, but they did not allow children."

Carol shared Etta's description of smuggling Carol into the camp. In an interview with Carol's daughter, Etta explained, "So I had that bag, and we put the baby in the bag, and we put clothes on top of it, and we took her into the labor camp on [Ignatz's] back. We walked into that labor camp. [Carol] was a baby. How could she understand anything? She didn't cry or say a word; she was amazing. So we took her into the camp. And what do we do now? We needed a hiding place for her. There was an attic, and we left her in there. My husband had to go to work. How could we leave the baby alone? She was alone all day in there with a piece of bread and a little water all day long.

"One day," Carol explained, "Mother was sick and couldn't go to work. The Nazi soldiers stomped up the stairs. There was an inspection, and there was no time to put me back in the attic. She wrapped a blanket around me and put me under the bed. The Gestapo came in with a huge German Shepherd; they hit my mother and asked her why she was not at work; the German Shepherd smelled me and lunged at me. Mother had told me to be quiet, but I started screaming and shaking, and they pulled me out. My mother said to them if you are going to kill us, kill me first. Anyway, for whatever reason, they turned around and walked out and never said anything."

While in the camp, Etta became pregnant again and had a little boy. Unfortunately, it was impossible to keep him in the camp. Etta and Ignatz had a gut-wrenching decision to make. If they kept the baby, he and Carol would undoubtedly be discovered, in which case, both children would be killed or subjected to torturous medical experiments. The second option was to allow their fellow inmates to provide a quick death to their newborn little boy and try to keep Carol hidden and alive. They chose option two.

They moved out of Boryslav and into Waldenburg after the Russians liberated the camp, "but it was during the Stalinist regime. It was like out of the frying pan and into the fire. People were taken away every day and shot, and the killings continued." Being liberated after World War II meant continued horrors for millions of refugees in Eastern Europe. "Most had nowhere to go, no food, nothing. We were given an apartment in Waldenburg; I am not sure why. Our lives were [still] in danger, and my father decided that we needed to get out of there, and we paid a smuggler a lot of money to smuggle us across the border into Czechoslovakia, where we hoped to make our way to some kind of safe place. We took only the clothes on our backs and whatever documents we needed. I had a new brother, and he was about eighteen months old. Mother put him in a carriage, and we took a walk to the edge of the woods at night. We left the carriage and everything and walked all night like the refugees today. We didn't even know if the guy would take us alive. Some smugglers took the money and shot the people they were escorting across the border … (As before in the work camp) the guy said to my mother, 'You can't take that baby; if he cries, they will kill all of us.' He wanted to suffocate my brother. And Mother said 'No!' and wouldn't let him. They gave my brother sleeping pills. But he didn't sleep; he was awake all night; my mother carried him all night, and he didn't make a sound until we arrived safely in Czechoslovakia." From Czechoslovakia, the family traveled by cattle car, walked many miles, and finally reached a refugee camp in the American Sector of Ulm, Germany. "In the American sector, we were finally safe."

When asked how her family could emotionally survive such horrors, Carol continues, "Every time my father wanted to face the dark side, my mother would pull him out of that. When we were in the ghetto, and I was hidden in the attic, my father [had procured] poison. A lot of people were poisoning their children, their families rather than having them suffer. He was able to get poison from a friend of his who was a pharmacist, and my mother said, 'No! We are either all going to die or all going to survive. I am not going to kill the baby.' She always pulled away from that whenever she could."

"Mom passed on to me strength and wisdom. She could have been broken, my father was, and she talks about that... how he couldn't take it. He was broken, and she had to be strong for both of them. There wasn't a night when he didn't cry. I remember my father being a broken man; he never got it back together again." Etta once said, "He couldn't stand it that he lost his family. He lost everything. 'Why am I alive? Why am I alive?' he cried. He never stopped crying. And he got sick, and he had heart attacks."

When I asked Carol to describe Etta, she said, "She was the one who took charge. When she got to the US, she got a job, he also worked, but she went hunting for a job, she became successful at it, she became a manager, she worked at a supermarket without knowing English [at first]. She also made sure that I got everything that I needed. I wanted to go to college, and my father didn't think that it was necessary. My father was so afraid; he was a very anxious man and afraid of everything. He couldn't stand it if he couldn't see where I was. I wanted to move away from home, and he was beside himself, and my mother said, 'No!' She has to go.'"

Etta made sure that her children got a good education. Her son has a PhD and is an eminent art historian, and Carol has an MSW and LCSW. "Mother had very little education, no more than sixth grade, but she made sure we got an education." When Carol graduated from college, she had a degree in journalism but was interested in science and worked in a research lab doing electron microscopy. She was studying aging and Alzheimer's from a cellular perspective. Then she went to graduate school in social work and turned to gerontology, working with Alzheimer's patients. She went from the lab to the clinical and ultimately to her own private practice. When she began her own practice, she worked with families and trauma, especially Post Traumatic Stress Disorder. I asked Carol her secret to aging gracefully and well, and her answer was, "Stay engaged, have people in your life, and read."

I asked Carol about the legacies that she was left by her parents; she said, "[Mother's] philosophy of life is one of my great legacies. She knew how to move on. Etta explained her ability to move forward in her life. 'It's all in the past, my dear. It's all that I'm thinking. I feel for the whole; I feel sorry that I lost my family. And I'm alone, and it's a little uncomfortable, but you have to get used to that kind of life too. It's no other choice. Whatever it is, you have to face it. That's all.'"

Carol believes that Etta's strength was passed down to her by her grandfather, who had "an attitude of positivity that was always there in my mother's life."

Even though her father was broken, Carol always knew that she was loved. "My father had a wonderful sense of humor. That's his legacy to me, his sense of humor." Carol also described her father's love of culture, love of art, intellect, and love of literature. She did two things together with her father. Once a week, they would go to the second-hand bookstore, and they also visited art museums together. Etta and Ignatz loved each other very much, and that love was passed down to their children.

Etta was only fifty-nine when Ignatz died from a stroke. Carol thought, "My mother is a poor old woman, and I am going to move her into my house. So we built an addition to my house so she could move in. Well, that lasted maybe a year, and then she said, 'I am going to Israel.' She had two brothers who had gone to Israel. So she went to Israel to visit them, and the next thing I knew, she had bought a condo in Jerusalem." Etta began dating again. "She had so many boyfriends; she was beautiful. Then she began ballroom dancing." Etta was in her sixties when she began dancing and kept dancing into her eighties. She went dancing every night. Carol once visited her when she was living in Miami Beach, and Carol could not keep up with her. It was this story of the smiling, dancing, eighty-year-old Etta, who found a way to embrace life even after living through unbearable horrors that captivated me forty years ago and encouraged me during the trials I faced in my own life.

Life is full of tragedy. We cannot escape death, disease (including global pandemics), economic insecurity, loss of relationships, and man's inhumanity to man. All of us are equally vulnerable. Some of us cannot find the strength to recover. The resilient Etta Hauptman and her family show the rest of us that recovery is possible, forgiveness is possible, love is possible, and even joy is possible, no matter what catastrophic losses you may have suffered. I am grateful to have heard Etta's story so many years ago.

Quotes from Etta:

On Jews and gentiles:

"Now tell me one thing. What's the difference? It's just a religion; it's nothing. The human being is the same. They talk like I talk; they walk like I walk; we are the same people."

On being grateful:

"We were happy; we were a happy family. Whatever we had, a piece of bread and butter and coffee, that was enough for us. We were happy with that. We didn't need luxuries; we didn't have any electricity. I remember when I was a kid... we used to chop up wood for light. The people were satisfied; we were satisfied. And now, all this luxury, I can't stand it. It's good to have a good family and have each other. It's more important than anything else. I would be satisfied with a piece of bread and butter for the rest of my life. Just to be satisfied with my family and to be loved."

On life goals:
"I wanted to be educated, I wanted to go to school, I wanted more than anything to be a mensch. [A decent person].

Later in life, when she had difficulty seeing, Etta said, *"Now I can't even see to write my name. Well, I am grateful to God that I can see [at all]. I can see people; I can see everything but not to read. So, I have to face that; I have to be satisfied with that and thank God for that. Like my father used to say, 'My child, when you go into the street, and you fall and break a leg, you have to thank God you didn't break both legs.'"*

Resources:

Man's Search for Meaning by Victor E. Frankl.

Resilient: Restoring Your Weary Soul in These Turbulent Times by John Eldredge.

Resilience: Hard-Won Wisdom for Living a Better Life by Eric Greitens.

https://www.mayoclinic.org/tests-procedures/resilience -training/in-depth/resilience/art-20046311.

https://www.psychologytoday.com/us/basics/resilience.

The Legacy of Laughter

*If you don't learn to laugh at trouble, you won't
have anything to laugh at when you're old.*
—Edgar Watson Howe

One of the legacies left to me by my mother, husband, and son
was the legacy of laughter. All three had a wicked sense of humor.
Mom was a traditional humorist, and Jim's humor focused on
adventure (and frequently was much funnier years later), while
Eric was just continuously hilarious. Once I was able to work
through the grief of their deaths, thinking about them makes
me smile. What a beautiful gift they left for me.

We can all think of wonderful comedians that made us laugh
through the years. As I mentioned earlier, when I was five, my
mom played the Danny Kaye song "I am Five." It was a unique
reminder of my mom's sense of humor. I played it for each of
my grandchildren when they turned five. Lucille Ball, Carol
Burnett, Steve Martin, and Robin Williams were my favorite
comedians. But you do not need to be famous to leave a similar
legacy to the people you love. Teach them to look at the humorous side of life even in a world full of chaos.

Speaking of chaos, getting old is the pits. Every joint hurts, we
need glasses to read, and many of the words that used to be at our
beck and call have left the building. (One of my motivations for
writing this book now is that I know it will be harder to write next

year.) Jim was the twelfth of fourteen children, and I was seven years younger than Jim. When I get together with the wider family (over half are now in their eighties), we spend a lot of time laughing! We help each other with our words in a continuous game of charades when we forget a common noun or verb. If one of us comes up with a forgotten word, we celebrate with high fives. Sometimes we resort to looking it up on our phones, followed by an equally celebrative ahh when the lost word is finally found. Interestingly, a Brookings Institute study shows that happiness peaks early in life and then in old age.[8] I think a big part of that happiness comes from being able to laugh at ourselves.

I only know one stand-up comedian personally, but she's a doozy! She may not be nationally known or outrageously wealthy, nonetheless, Rosemond "Rosie" Sarpong Owens is a force of nature! Rosie uses laughter to accomplish her goals related to work and service in a way I have never seen before. I first met Rosie when she was the president of Books for Africa. She was leading a fundraising effort, and I was captivated. Rosie possesses a stunning presence. She is from Kumasi, Ghana, and dresses in colorful African clothing. Her hair is arranged beautifully, frequently interwoven with a sensational scarf. Her real gift is humor. Somehow Rosie has the ability to command a room to do things they might not be ready to do (like give up their money) and then be happy they did it. It's mesmerizing to watch her. For years I have been trying to figure out her secret, and all I can come up with is that it must be a mysterious combination of authenticity, a gigantic, beautiful smile, a memorable and melodious voice, and continuous humor. Her Ghanaian accent doesn't hurt. Fortunately for the world, she uses her superpowers for good!

For her day job, Rosie is raising her daughters and serves a

---

[8] www.healthy.kaiserpermanente.org.

large health care company as their Racial and Health Equity Practitioner. At night she does stand-up comedy.

Rosie grew up in Ghana; her mother and father taught her the value of working hard, her mom was a business woman, and her father was a "serial entrepreneur." "He woke up at 5:00 a.m. every day. He was always trying to do better. He was the epitome of hard work... he put a full day in, and he loved farming. He used to raise animals. My dad didn't feel that a human being should be in bed after the sun rises. Even now, I can't sleep in; I don't know how to do that. That's what I learned from my dad."

Rosie became interested in humor at an early age. "I think I was always funny.. That is how I was created; God made me funny." Rosie felt that humor was not appreciated in her community growing up, and people equated humor with someone being a buffoon or a fool. They did not see humor as something good. Later, Rosie found that humor was tied to the gift of encouragement.

Rosie met her future husband, Isaac, as a college student in Ghana. "He lived from Minnesota, but he came for a visit." Rosie remembers, "He was the brother of my roommate, Mercy, in college. Isaac is very easygoing and decent and very warm. Our families had known each other for a long time." After college, they went their separate ways, Mercy (who is currently a physician in Great Britain), brought them together again. Isaac was flying, at the time in Germany, and he visited her while Rosie was studying in Spain. "And then," according to Rosie, "the rest is history." Isaac was just what Rosie needed. "Isaac was different. He was always supportive of me, I am a lot of things, and Isaac supported them all!"

When Rosie was in high school, everyone knew she was funny. When her friends were feeling sad, they would come to her for encouragement. Her nickname was "Rosie Posey" because she made people feel better.

She was once speaking at a bioterrorism conference around 9/11. Rosie was talking about security and birth certificates. It was a serious conference and a serious topic. Everyone was tense. "From the time I got on the stage until the time I left, people didn't stop laughing." It didn't even dawn on Rosie why she was so funny, but in the bathroom after the conference (where many important discussions take place), women were asking her if she did stand-up comedy. Later, she got a message from an old friend from school who she hadn't seen for years. When she spoke to her friend, the friend said, "Rosie, I have been looking for you for years, and I have been sick for a long time, and I always remembered how you made me feel, and I was looking for you because I knew that you could make me feel better." This was a revelation for Rosie; they began to talk regularly. Rosie has a circle of amazing classmates from the Wesley School in Ghana that keep in touch regularly, and Rosie invited this woman in. Through the intervention of a physician in the group, the woman is doing much better. This event caused Rosie to realize the importance of encouragement and the relationship of laughter to encouragement and to healing. Rosie considers laughter, encouragement, and joy her gift to give. Whenever someone randomly comes to her mind, she reaches out to them. (I have to admit that I have been the beneficiary of her encouraging texts.)

Once, Rosie had the strange feeling that she should call an old friend who used to work for the United Nations. It took her a while, but she was finally able to track that friend down. The woman responded to Rosie's call with, "How did you know?" Her fiancé had just broken up with her, and she was stuck alone in a hotel in Nigeria and feeling very sad. Rosie's sixth sense had struck again!

Rosie calls herself a CEO–chief encouragement officer. She spreads her encouragement to university students as she speaks to them frequently. She wants to help them and give them a sense of worth. Her motto is that you leave people better than you found them. I can tell you from personal experience that Rosie is an astounding success at accomplishing that goal.

Several months before his death, former Secretary General of the United Nations, Kofi Annan, spoke to a gathering of Books for Africa supporters. Rosie was asked to host the meeting, but it was suggested that she somewhat suppress her normal enthusiasm in deference to the Secretary General. Rosie did not listen; she was her normal hilarious self. A few weeks later, she received a letter from Kofi Annan thanking her and asserting, "Your lively and colorful presence animated the whole evening."

"For those of us who have children or grandchildren," Rosie explained, "a critical piece is being open for people to explore who they are; we need to nurture that. Once there is breath in you, there is purpose in who you are and what you bring. When I was in Ghana, children were taught to be something they are not. When I was in school, I was taught to quit talking and quit laughing. I thank God that after all of that, I became who I was destined to be. I think that our world needs young women who are strong. Society does itself a disservice when it looks down on humor. Life is tough. People who are able to bring joy are like rays of sunshine. We need people who can bring out the joy in us."

We need more people like Rosie Sarpong.

Laughing at oneself is a unique talent that I hope to pass on to my grandchildren. As a speaker, I learned that if I made a mistake on stage, the audience would be much more accepting if I was able to laugh at myself. Understanding and accepting yourself as a flawed human being and finding humor in that is freeing. It is important to discern the difference between laughing at yourself in a healthy manner with wholesome self-esteem and putting yourself down in a demeaning way, which is definitely not healthy.

Jim and I gave ourselves a lot of material to laugh about! One of our favorite places to visit was my birthplace, Carmel-by-the-Sea,

California. Carmel has beautiful beaches, wonderful restaurants, amazing artists, and splendid golf courses. The people were typically friendly and hospitable. Except on one occasion when they weren't! Jim and I were visiting a golf course in the area (I won't reveal the name–it doesn't matter), and decided to have lunch. We walked up to the hostess and waited for a table. The hostess ignored us. At first, we thought she was just busy, although there were empty tables visible. It was as if we were invisible; there was no acknowledgment that we were there. A few minutes later, a pleasant, attractive young couple walked up behind us and took their place in line. The hostess headed towards us. At last, we would get our table! But instead of taking our names, she walked around us and asked the couple behind us if they wanted a table. The couple, obviously embarrassed, said, "Oh, no. These people were here first."

The hostess, who now seemed quite irritated with our presence, said, "Oh, okay," and took us to a table. The rest of our visit went very well. Our waitress was fabulous, and the food was great. After lunch, we walked across the parking lot to our car. An expensive red convertible sped around us and parked. As the three occupants, one young man and two young women, walked past us, we could hear the young man shout out loudly, "Nerd Alert!" Jim and I were the only people in the parking lot. At first, we were shocked and confused. What did he mean? And then we looked at each other and started laughing, uncontrollably. What the young man didn't know was that the joke was on him. We were nerds and proud of it! We were from a small Minnesota town and were proud of it. We were old and did not spend much money on our clothes and were proud of it! I don't think the young man was expecting our reaction; now, he was the one who looked confused. He may have been trying to put us down, but we were laughing at ourselves with the understanding that we were happy nerds, and that was okay with us! Don't ever let anyone else define who you are. My mother taught me that.

Author J.K. Rowling at her 2008 Harvard Commencement address, said, "The first thing I would like to say is 'thank you.' Not only has Harvard given me an extraordinary honor, but the weeks of fear and nausea I have endured at the thought of giving this commencement address have made me lose weight. A win-win situation!"[9]

Only a brilliant author with healthy self-esteem would choose to connect with her audience through words such as fear, nausea, and weight loss.

Laughter is healthy. According to the Mayo Clinic, "When it comes to relieving stress, more giggles and guffaws are just what the doctor ordered."[10] In fact, laughter increases your consumption of oxygen and can decrease stress. We all know that laughter decreases mental pain, but since mental and physical pain is closely related, laughter can reduce physical pain. Who knew?

I discovered the healing power of laughter during some of my darkest times. Years ago, during one of Jim's "almost dead" events, his sisters provided me with emotional support in a most peculiar and unusual way.

Jim was recovering from a quadruple bypass and valve replacement at the Mayo Clinic, and things were not going well. Jim was struggling, and his oxygen saturation levels (a measure of how efficiently the lungs are oxygenating the blood) were too low. His doctors ordered that the nasal cannula he was using be replaced with a mask to ensure more oxygen would go to his lungs. Jim did not like wearing masks and had somehow convinced his nurse that if she turned his bed around so that he

---

[9]   News.harvard.edu.

[10]   Mayoclinic.org, "Stress relief from laughter is no joke."

could see his saturation levels, he would breathe in more deeply and raise them to an acceptable point. He was also getting ready to take a nap, and I, in a frustrated tone, pointed out the flaw in this proposal; if he was asleep, he would not be able to see his saturation levels. Jim was unmoved and insisted that his plan would work even as he slept. Exasperated at his logic, I mumbled something like, "I am not going to stand here and watch you die of stubbornness," and stomped out of the room in tears. A few minutes later, I realized that even if he died of stubbornness, I wanted my last words to him to be loving, not angry.

When I returned to Jim's room, I was relieved to see that his bed had been moved back into the correct position, and he was now wearing the full face mask. Crisis averted!

A bit later, Jim's sisters, Judy, Sue, and Lois, came for a visit. They entered the room and greeted us in their typical jovial style. I, however, was not in a jovial mood, and I didn't want Jim to use his energy and limited oxygen to talk. I wanted him to breathe!

I expressed my concern to the sisters, expecting sympathy. I did not get sympathy. Judy's answer to my distress still rings in my ears over ten years later. With a smile and a twinkle in her eye, Judy's response to my alarm over her brother's oxygenation levels was, "Oh, Kim, stop being such a witch." But she did not say witch. She used a word that rhymes with witch but begins with a *b*.

You may be surprised that I describe this event in my chapter on laughter. To understand this story, you have to understand who Judy is. She is the ultimate church lady. I have never, before this incident, heard her swear. In the over forty years that I had been married to her brother, she had never even admonished me. For her to call me such a name at this place and at this time was a complete shock. Her response was uncharacteristic, unexpected, confounding, and surprising, and caused a full emotional reset in my brain. It was like a slap in the face to reset someone who is hysterical. Because of our trusting relationship and Judy's funny body language, facial expression, and tone, it was hysterically funny.

I started laughing uncontrollably.

Judy, Sue, and Lois started laughing too. Eventually, even Jim started laughing. The sisters' visit was a Godsend and set both Jim and me at ease. When Jim was wheeled away to have his lungs drained, and I started worrying again, Judy or Lois would interject an unexpected "witch" into the conversation, and we would all burst out laughing. The lung draining did the trick, and Jim's recovery began.

A few years later, there was another close call. Jim was suffering septic shock, on a ventilator, in an induced coma, and had just endured a heart attack. Lois called to see how he was doing, and I was in a bad state. After describing his condition and poor prognosis, I cried out on the phone, "Lois, I think I need someone to call me a witch!" She complied, and we laughed through our tears. I believe that when you combine laughter with sorrow, it becomes sacred. Thank you, Lois and Judy and Sue, for the gift of sacred laughter.

Sacred laughter is a memorable event. I have experienced it with my "Mommas" group (women who have all lost sons to suicide), my church grief support group, with my widow's group, and with individual friends as we suffered through sorrow. I am convinced that the combination of laughter and tears experienced with someone else has magical healing powers.

Resources:
Laughter Yoga by Madan Kataria.
Apples in a Seed: Unleashing the Unique You by Rosemond Sarpong Owens.
https://mrfeelgood.com/articles/the-best-medicine-laughter.

The Legacy of Encouragement

*Be an Encourager: When you encourage others, you boost
their self-esteem, enhance their self-confidence, make them
work harder, lift their spirits, and make them successful in
their endeavors. Encouragement goes straight to the heart
and is always available. Be an encourager. Always.*
—Roy T. Bennett, The Light in the Heart

I have been blessed by an army of encouragers like Rosie. The
first one was my mother. My grandmothers also played an encouraging role. I lost my encouragers at home when I transitioned to
my father and stepmother's house. Fortunately, my 4-H leader,
Mrs. Brown, stepped into that role in middle and high school.
When I was seventeen, I met my husband Jim, who became my
chief encourager until his death forty-six years later. Little did
we know that in year thirty-three of our marriage, we would face
one of the most significant encouragement challenges known to
humankind: losing a child.

On the evening of January 31, 2009, my husband Jim and I
were in Washington, DC, for a business meeting and had just
finished a wonderful dinner with old friends. My dental school
lab partner, Ron Hauptman, was driving us back to our hotel,
and I checked my phone to see if I had received any messages
while at dinner. There were eight. My heart sank as the first one
was from a police officer, a patient of mine, from our hometown

of Farmington, Minnesota. I called him back immediately. His first words were, "Where are you now?" I told him. He asked if I was driving. I said no. He then said that he was sorry to have to tell me this news over the phone, but police officers had been dispatched to our hotel, The Hay Adams, and they could not find us. He then said that he had received a call from a police officer in New York that our son, a student at Columbia University, had died by suicide. Our precious son Eric was dead.

My heart stopped for a moment and then shattered into a thousand pieces. I cried out to my husband that Eric was dead. He said, "Which Eric?" He was unable to comprehend that it could be his son. "Our Eric," I told him. At that moment, we shared a formerly incomprehensible understanding of the depths of despair and grief. I can hardly remember the rest of that night or the rest of that month. I had to call my two daughters, Hillary and Ashley. They were in shock. Their screams and cries ring in my ears even today. Ron took care of us, helped us check out of our hotel, and put us on a train to New York. The student services staff at Columbia were wonderful. They picked us up from the airport, gave us a place to stay, and took us to the police station and then to the morgue. Never could we have imagined that we would have to confirm our son's identity in a New York City morgue. Eric's death became real to us at that moment. He looked so sad. He seemed so cold. He was no longer with us, and we would never see him in this world again.

Two weeks before, when Eric had returned to New York, he was happier than we had ever seen him. He loved Columbia, and Columbia loved him. Eric was studying engineering and made the dean's list his first semester. He wanted to be a patent attorney and bought books before he left, comparing law schools. The day before he left, he was filling out internship applications for the summer. He went to Columbia because he wanted to study jazz piano along with engineering. He had been admitted into their jazz program as a jazz pianist. His jazz professor told us that Eric's enthusiasm inspired him to love teaching again. He had so much fun teaching Eric that his half-hour lessons frequently lasted over an hour. He also made a name for himself in theater and drew critical acclaim for his acting abilities. Eric had formed a new group for engineers who loved Latin. They would get together and quote their favorite Latin writers. Eric's was Cicero. Eric also represented his engineering class on the student council. Although several people ran against him, Eric was noted for his character and as a candidate who refused to participate in negative campaigning. He won his position by a wide margin. All of this occurred in just five months. The dean of the engineering school said that he had never known of a student making such a positive impact on a school in five short months. In high school, Eric also made an impression. He was brilliant, a National Merit Scholar. He participated on several academic teams at the state and national levels and even set a school record of five National Latin Gold Medals. He was a leader, the senior drum major, the jazz combo leader, and the student producer in theater. He did very well in sports but gave it up for music and theater. He was also active in our youth group at church and was one of the youngest members of our worship team. But most of all, at Columbia and in high school, Eric was known for his quirky, funny personality and his humility, kindness, and compassion. If someone needed a friend, Eric was there. If someone needed help, Eric was there. Eric touched more lives with love and compassion in his nineteen years on earth than most people in ninety.

Why would such a wonderful young man with such a bright future and many people who loved him choose to end his life? We will never know or understand. It does appear that Eric acted impulsively and quickly, and his death occurred within an hour after a final breakup with his girlfriend. It doesn't appear that he wanted to die. He called several people for help for thirty minutes, but everything that could go wrong did go wrong, and his life ended just as rescuers arrived.

During this time, in the depths of our most profound grief, we learned the importance of the legacy of encouragement. Anyone who has lost a child can tell you there are no words to describe the pain. It is unfathomable. But friends, family, professional colleagues, and our church held us up and walked beside us. It was one of the greatest legacies we have ever experienced and essential to our ability to move forward. Help from people who share your faith is particularly helpful when dealing with life-and-death issues.

The next week was a blur. My biggest concern was my husband and daughters. Jim had just survived cancer and a liver transplant. Hillary and Ashley were very close to Eric and were devastated. We could barely function. Our family and friends held us up. Jim's sister, Sylvia, moved in for the week, ensuring we ate something, putting us to bed, and feeding those who gathered at our home. Friends and family comforted us, held us up, and cared for all the details. My book club friends worked with Eric's high school band instructor, and his theater director made additional DVDs and arranged for the jazz band and concert band to perform at his funeral. Eric was no longer a student at St. Thomas, a Catholic all boy's military academy, but they treated him like he was still there. His funeral was at noon on a school day, but several busloads of students, including the honor guard, came in their dress uniforms to honor him. The funeral was amazing. We all cried as Eric's former classmates saluted his casket. Most of his teachers and school administrators came as well. Our church pastors were wonderful. Over

1500 people attended his funeral in Minnesota. Several other memorials were held at Columbia.

Jim and I had never realized how many friends we had. Every day we were held up by someone. Our grief was shared by many. We met others who had lost a loved one to suicide. A friend connected us to a couple who had lost their son a year before. As it turned out, my daughter, Ashley, attended the same Illinois college and knew his roommate well. They prayed with us, and through their example, we had hope that eventually, through God's help, healing would come. Eventually, this contact led to the formation of a support group of mothers who had lost their sons to suicide. We called ourselves "The Mommas" and met for several years.

The week after Eric's death, we received a letter from Linden Dungy, a dentist practicing a few blocks away from our office. He had lost his nephew, Jamie, to suicide at about the same age and under circumstances very similar to Eric's death. He wrote, "I did not know your son Eric, but my understanding is that he confessed a personal relationship with Jesus Christ. Two things come to mind. First, I do not know what your journey going forward will be like now, but there is one who does know. The Lord not only knows how you feel but had to endure the separation from His son."

Linden's words struck a deep chord. Although the fog that encompassed us in those first days was heavy and seemingly never-ending, through the help of our friends such as Linden, our family, and the pastors at Berean Baptist Church, Jim and I began to see glimmers of light and hope. We had no idea how wide a net of support we had and how wonderfully they seemed to know just what we needed and just what to say to us. We felt completely helpless, unable to sleep or eat. Making decisions seemed impossible. Just as we began to make progress emotionally, waves of grief would overwhelm us, and we would fall back into deep despair. We couldn't understand what had happened.

We couldn't believe that this had happened. How could we have lost our precious son? How could God have let this happen? Where was Eric? Would we see him again? How could we ever manage to live without him? As we struggled to get back to some sense of normalcy, we began to see God's healing hand. Unfortunately, this was not my first brush with suicide. Not only had my dear mother taken her life when I was seventeen, my nephew, Zachary, a brilliant student and PhD candidate, also took his life by jumping off a tall building in Japan just as he was finishing his degree. As a teenager, suffering severe depression, I attempted to take my life as well. But never in my wildest dreams did I think my beautiful boy was at risk. Although he struggled to fit in for many years, as do so many other brilliant people, he had been accepted and loved for his kindness and compassion as well as his unusual sense of humor both in high school and in college.

For the last several years of his life, he had been a great success at everything that he did, especially when it came to reaching out to those in need of a friend. Eric was loved by his family and friends and teachers. What went wrong? How could he ever have gotten to the point where he thought that life was not worth living?

In the months that followed, I was particularly worried about Ashley. She was just starting her second semester at the University of St. Thomas School of Law in Minneapolis. She was in shock and couldn't absorb what she was reading. This is not a good development for a law student. She missed school the week after Eric died and the following week when we went to Columbia, so she had much catching up to do. Ashley desperately tried to keep up and spent her entire spring break in the St. Thomas library! There was just one class she could not catch up with as there were several assignments due when she was gone. The professor of that class did an astonishing thing. She worked with Scott Swanson from the advising office and told Ashley that she could drop the class and take it as a tutorial in the summer. What a beautiful and thoughtful gesture! Because of Professor McGuigan, Ashley was able to complete her freshman year on time and begin her second year with the rest of her class. We will always be grateful to Ashley's law school family for understanding the special needs of a traumatized student.

About a week after Eric's death, my niece, Sarah, sent me a book, *Quiet Strength*, written by Linden's brother, Super Bowl-winning coach, international speaker, and bestselling author, Tony Dungy. Tony gave the world a great gift in this book in many ways, but for me, his frank discussion about the death of his son, Jamie, was life changing. Tony said that he would never understand why Jamie died, and he accepted that. He also said that he had to accept the fact that God had a plan that was bigger than we know, and we had to trust in His goodness and His mercy. I believe in that truth.

Linden prayed for us, met with us every Tuesday for lunch, and wrote us letters using God's words to comfort us. God gave him just the right words. Many times in those early days, as I struggled with specific issues, Linden's letter addressed just that issue.

One day at work, I had a massive meltdown in the stairwell. Several wonderful employees attempted to comfort me, but I was a wreck as I coped with trying to understand where Eric was. Suddenly, my office manager came running in and said, "Linden just delivered this." All of Linden's other letters had been sent through the mail, but this time Linden told me that he had a compelling feeling that he needed to deliver this message right away. I opened the letter, and the first thing I saw was a quote that stopped my meltdown in its tracks. Linden had highlighted Romans 8:38, "*For I am convinced that neither death nor life, neither angels nor demons, neither the present nor the future, nor any powers, neither height nor depth nor anything else in all creation, will be able to separate us from the love of God that is in Christ Jesus our Lord.*" My question about Eric's whereabouts was answered. How did Linden know?

When Jim and I realized that we were coping with Eric's loss in very different ways, Linden shared, "The best and most important thing that we could do was commit to being there for each other. To support each other to understand that each person was going to need understanding, versus trying to fix each other, and to commit to the concept of whatever it was going to take, whatever was going to be needed, that they would be there for one another as a couple, not as two people trying to cope by themselves."

When we struggled to get back to life and attend our first wedding, Linden wrote, "Yes, I am saddened that I will not see my nephew grow up, get married, raise a family, and grow old with his cousins. I can imagine that you had similar hopes and aspirations for your son Eric. But on this day, I will celebrate the resurrection with you; I will celebrate with you that special time we see all of our loved ones again and provide the evidence that God's word is truth and that hope in God is not in vain."

One of the barriers to finding God's joy again after such a catastrophic loss is the guilt associated with any possibility of happiness without your loved one. How could we ever be happy without our precious son? Would our acceptance of joy dishonor his memory? Linden wrote on March 9, "It may feel like moving on, looking to the future is a total disregard for Eric and the life he had. It is okay to move forward while hanging onto your memories. Eric has passed out of our time and space into God's eternity, but remember that God is the God of the living, not the dead. Remember that Eric still lives, just like the scriptures tell us about Abraham, Isaac, and Jacob still living."

For several months, our Tuesday meetings seemed like extremely effective counseling sessions. But after a while, as Jim and I began to heal, we began to talk about Linden's family and his professional goals. We were able to help him with some issues regarding a new office and shared our experiences in that area. We marveled at God's goodness in placing such a wonderful man right down the street from us.

Jim and I were also blessed by our pastors, who took calls from us regularly in the first days after Eric's death. Pastor Boyd wrote and performed a song for Eric, and Pastor Thompson, who was always there with just the right book or Bible passage, made a beautiful shadow box for us. Eric was even honored at our church's Vacation Bible School, where Eric worked for years in the music and drama departments.

Although we are Baptists, Eric went to a Catholic school. The St. Thomas Academy community could not have been more supportive. We were blessed by the kindnesses and memories of Eric's former schoolmates, teachers, and administrators. A few weeks after Eric's death, we received a letter from Archbishop Flynn: "The breaking of any human circle demands a certain tribute of tears, and when that circle is broken by the death of someone so young, in circumstances that are mysterious, then the tears become more plentiful and the pain more poignant. However, we are people who believe in God, and we are people who believe that death does not cancel out any one of us and that death is a call to live in the life of our God. Therefore, let your son, Eric be in God. Let him be in God's life. Let him be in God's love."

Life's journey involves many joys and many sorrows. The loss of my son has opened my heart and consciousness to many sorrows that I did not comprehend before. I now understand what it means to lose an only son and God's sacrifice on our behalf. I understand at a much deeper level the miracle of Easter and that

Christ's death on the cross opened the gates of heaven to my son and gave me the hope to see him again. And I understand that God is merciful and is here with me, providing me with His love and the love of wonderful friends and family who have held me up during this time of trial. It is my hope that I can also use my experience to help others who are facing similar trials.

Eric's classmates planted a tree and plaque for him at Columbia. It is a shadbush that will grow eighteen feet wide. The shadbush is a giving tree and was chosen to represent Eric's giving ways and big hugs that he gave out so freely and so often. His classmates at St. Thomas Academy planted an oak tree for Eric on their campus and placed a bench and a plaque to honor him. Although Eric was a young man with an incredibly brilliant mind and unique talents, he is remembered by his peers for his huge heart, generosity, and compassion. I could not be prouder.

God does not promise us a life without trials, grief, or catastrophic losses. He does promise us that he is with us, grieving for us, and holding us in the palm of His hand. In our case, God provided many angels in the form of family and friends who helped us survive, move forward, and work to find God's purpose in our lives. I believe that Eric's short nineteen years of life and tragic death contained many lessons for us all. It opened up many discussions about the grief, depression, and despair suffered by young men, particularly after a failed relationship. Eric lived a life of great love and service to others and touched many lives through his love. Eric had everything to live for, but ultimately, lost his focus over the grief of one failure. In the end, he lost his life on Earth, and we lost his presence in our lives. How often do we allow one failed relationship, loss of a job, or loss of a loved one to throw us into grief that will enable us to forget all that we have to live for? I hope that, in the end, we can all learn through God's grace to live by Eric's example (living and loving life to the fullest) and learn by his mistake (allowing one failure to blot out all of the joys life has to offer). The legacy of encouragement, of being there for others, is one of the greatest gifts you can give. We are all on this earth together, and our most significant purpose is to support each other in our triumphs and console each other through tragedy.

Resources:

Quiet Strength by Tony Dungy.

Uncommon by Tony Dungy.

God Is Always With You: 31 Days of Hope and Healing for Grief and Loss by The Team at LifeSupport Resources.

The Healing Name of Jesus by Jenita Pace.

The Legacy of Peace

Blessed are the peacemakers, for they
will be called children of God.
—Matthew 5:9 NIV

I was ecstatic when my daughter, Hillary, brought me out of retirement to serve as a dental consultant for her dental law firm. I could now use the thirty-plus years of training and experience in a field I loved to help my daughter build her practice. Later she brought my other daughter, Ashley, into the firm to serve Kansas and Missouri. I now work with both of my daughters. (A reality that would have horrified them as teenagers.) When my children were young, Jim and I had hoped that one of them would follow our lead and enter the field of dentistry, with our goal of one day handing over the practice we built to them. Both girls made it clear that they were marching to their own drummer. It was our job, as parents, to facilitate their independent journey. They, instead, followed the mentorship of my dear friend, Sheryl Ramstad, and became attorneys. Little did I dream that my wish for a family business would be fulfilled and that I would work with not just one but both of my daughters, in an entirely different profession, with Hillary, not me, as the boss! God has a great sense of humor!

My role in the organization is to help the lawyers understand the details of the practice of dentistry. Both girls were introduced to the dental profession when they worked as teenagers and occasionally as college students at our practice. I also wanted to better understand the law, and I trained as a civil mediator. Later, I became a Qualified Neutral for the State of Minnesota (Minnesota-speak for a civil mediator). I found this area of peace-making very rewarding, and the training helped me immensely in my personal life.

We live in a hyper-polarized society. Families are torn apart, people are "canceled," and our politicians have less independence to make decisions outside of their party line than at any other time in my life, which at this writing, is sixty-six years! A 2014 PEW research article called "Political Polarization in the American Public"[11] describes the growing contempt one party has for the other in the US. Yikes! Contempt is a strong word!

This is not the first time one group within the same country has experienced "contempt" for another. It has happened in almost every continent. (Antarctica, perhaps, is excluded.) Some examples include Germany against the Jews, Turkey against the Armenians, and Rwanda against the Tutsis. All three ended up in horrific genocides. Hopefully, we in the US will come to our senses before we get that far.

I first understood what happens when one group wishes the other dead when my dental lab partner, Ron, explained the horrors of the Holocaust. (See "The Legacy of Resilience" chapter.) Those stories stayed with me for over forty years. When genocides occurred in my lifetime, including the one against the Tutsi in Rwanda in 1994, I was horrified but busy raising my family safely and securely in a small town, Farmington, Minnesota.

Trigger Warning: Genocide, mutilation, and other crimes against humanity.

---

[11] https://www.pewresearch.org/politics/2014/06/12/political-polarization-in-the-american-public/.

After Eric died, the story of Rwanda returned to me as I read books and met people who had survived. How could anyone survive genocide? What was their secret? I felt that, after the loss of my son, I would never be able to find emotional peace, much less joy, but here were people who had lost their entire families and everything they owned, and somehow they were rebuilding their lives with what remained. They created new families, built new homes, and, unbelievably, sought forgiveness and reconciliation towards those who savagely raped, tortured, and killed their loved ones.

I first visited Rwanda in 2012, eighteen years after almost one million people were killed in just one hundred days. My incredible friend and library partner, Pam Pappas Stanoch, and I were dedicating seven Eric Harms Memorial Libraries, including elementary, secondary, university, dental school, and law libraries. We were told before we left that it was politically incorrect to talk about the genocide, but when we got there, the genocide story came to us.

Fr. Reme Bizimani agreed to process our book shipments. He also served as our guide while we were in Rwanda. Shortly after the genocide began, when Reme was fifteen, a neighbor raced over to his house to tell his father that the killers were coming to wipe out his family. Reme's father felt there was not enough time to save his entire family, so he sent his two sons, Reme, and his younger brother, with the neighbor, who hid them in a wood bin. Reme and his brother stayed in that small bin for almost three months until the slaughter ended. When they emerged, they found that their father, mother, and five-year-old sister had been killed, probably the same day the boys went into hiding.

After the genocide, Reme and his brother were adopted by an aunt who was an Anglican Canon and his uncle, a Baptist pastor. His aunt and uncle had lost five of their seven children, and for eleven years, they thought they had also lost their infant granddaughter. In 2005 a prisoner confessed that the child had not been killed. Her parents, facing their killers, had the presence of mind to make a bargain. They would find and collect all of their money and exchange that for the life of their child. Once the money was given to the killers, the parents were brutally murdered. The baby was spared and given to a Hutu family to raise her. After several years of searching for the child, she was finally found living happily with the family who raised her. At fourteen, she was reunited with her grandparents and extended Tutsi family and now lives with both families. I cannot imagine the emotional complexities the young girl must face.

Father Reme and his family gave us the honor of taking us to the Murambi Genocide Memorial in southwest Rwanda. He had arranged a private tour for us. Our guide and three companions lost multiple family members in the genocide. Pam and I walked the narrow path on the grounds of a former technical college where forty-five thousand people were murdered on April 21, 1994. Tutsis and moderate Hutus who had tried to hide in a local church had been led to the school with promises of protection but instead were massacred.

Most were buried in mass graves, but to ensure that the world would never forget—or worse, deny—what had happened there, the remains of nearly one thousand victims had been preserved in lime. Guns and grenades had killed some, but the vast majority had been slashed to death with machetes. As a testimony to the effectiveness of this killing machine, only a handful of the forty-five thousand who sought refuge at Murambi survived. As might be expected, few survivors described how the killing of their friends and family was accomplished. But here, at Murambi, they did not have to. The final moments in the lives of these men, women, children, and infants were graphically evident. Arms and legs had been severed; skulls were crushed beyond recognition as human. Some had been buried alive among the corpses of their family members, their arms reaching out as if trying to find an escape. Many women who had been violated had foreign objects still protruding from their bodies. The visit to Murambi with these survivors was a great privilege, and one of the most sacred moments of my life. I will never forget it.

I will also never forget the Rwandan Collectives. Tutsi women whose husbands had been killed in the genocide had joined with Hutu women whose husbands had done the killing and were now in jail. They had put aside their differences and focused on forgiveness and reconciliation. These women realized they had much in common and focused on those commonalities. Each collective determined the type of work they would rely upon. Many made traditional crafts, sewing or weaving baskets. One of the collectives we visited in Musanze was trying to secure micro-loans to start a business that would distribute coal in their village more efficiently. These women were amazing. Pam and I bonded with them immediately.

There was, unexpectedly, much joy and laughter in these groups.

In Musanze, we were greeted with singing and dancing. When we were about to leave, the women began singing and dancing again and brought the two of us in to join them. I have to admit that I am not much of a dancer. In America, we dance for enjoyment and to be seen and show our talent. In the Rwandan collectives, they dance as an expression of joy. You could almost feel the joy coming out of the fingertips of these women. By the time we were done, I could feel the joy coming from my fingertips. Joy is contagious. With such a horrible past to work through and lives lived in such stark financial poverty, how could these Tutsi and Hutu women dance together with such joy?

Unimaginable peace is the legacy of Rwanda. I am unaware of any country that has recovered so quickly from such devastation.

On our 2012 visit, we were caught off guard by the number of prisoners in pink jumpsuits out in the field, growing their food or walking along the streets, single file, going peacefully back to their prison cells. Frequently we would see a long line of twenty or so prisoners with hoes, shovels, and other potential weapons walking between two armed guards. From my perspective, this seemed like a dangerous combination, but when asked about the danger, Fr. Reme just laughed. "The prisoners would not attack the guards," he said, "They have nowhere to go; their families would just turn them back in to the police!" Okay, then!

This peace was secured because the Rwandans thought beyond the human desire for revenge and looked to their children's future. They realized that if they kept the hatred and contempt alive, their children would likely live through the same atrocities they had suffered. Instead, they put their egos aside and sought justice, forgiveness, reconciliation, and peace.

Because of the emotional sacrifices made by Rwandans in the years following 1994, Rwanda is thriving. It is one of the safest countries in Africa, and, at this writing, Rwanda shares a US State Department rating of One: Exercise Normal Precautions, with Canada. If you are not worried about going to Canada, you shouldn't worry about going to Rwanda. Kigali is beautiful, with new skyscrapers going up every time I visit. There are great hotels and many excellent safari opportunities in Akagera National Park on the eastern border and the golden monkeys and mountain gorillas of Volcanoes National Park on the northern border.

Rwanda is seeing progress in the country's goal of providing clean water to its thirteen million people and progress in education and developing health care initiatives. When I first visited Rwanda in 2012, it had just graduated its first-ever class of dentally trained practitioners; dental therapists. With the help of Harvard University Dental School and my alma mater, the University of Maryland Dental School, they combined programs with the University of Rwanda School of Medicine and are now graduating dental surgeons. There is still a long way to go to provide access to care for most Rwandans, but they are making progress. When a country is at peace, it can focus on building opportunities. One of my favorite Rwandans is a young man named Fabrice. Pam and I met Fabrice on our first visit; even as a student, he was unique. Fabrice served as interpreter and technology whiz for his class. Later, when I came to lecture, Fabrice managed all the details, including transportation.

Fabrice became an orphan shortly after the genocide; then, he went to live with his aunt. When she died, his aunt's best friend, Bamurange Therese, adopted him. Her husband was killed during the genocide. After his death, she fled with her seven children. On several occasions, she met roadblocks where she was identified as Tutsi. Miraculously, someone recognized her each time and, because of her kind reputation, couldn't bring themselves to kill her. Instead, they recommended that she be sent to the next roadblock where another group would surely kill her and her children. Eventually, she made it out of the country. Bamurange is a fearless woman. Even after losing everything and with seven children to feed, she took in her friend's nephew, Fabrice. This legacy of selflessness is repeated again and again in Rwanda.

When Fabrice graduated as a dental therapist, he faced significant barriers to starting his own practice. The banks were unfamiliar with a dental practice outside of a hospital, so financing was unavailable. Equipment was hard to come by, and the laws changed as Rwanda evolved. Fabrice worked various jobs as a pharmaceutical representative and selling dental equipment. Finally, after almost eight years of struggle, he finally accomplished his dream of owning a dental practice! A year after opening, Fabrice's Urban Dental Clinic received a consumer choice award from a local newspaper. He has also started his own medical company: Kings Medical Ltd. Fabrice is now a husband, father, and award-winning entrepreneur. I am so proud to know him.

When we delivered our first libraries in 2012, two were law libraries donated by Thompson-Reuters. The Books for Africa Law and Democracy initiative was founded by former UN Secretary-General Kofi Annan and former US Vice President Walter Mondale to serve the needs of emerging democracies in Africa. We could visit the law school in Butare and interview the students there. They were excited about the new library because books, in general, and legal texts, in particular, were scarce. They were excited about their opportunities when they graduated and spoke of the severe shortage of lawyers (only forty left in the country) after the genocide. The lack of a legal system to oversee justice after the genocide promoted the formation of a community justice system or Gacaca courts to try those deemed responsible for the killings locally. The United Nations security council tried the high-ranking officials through the International Criminal Tribunal for Rwanda. Neither of these systems is without controversy, but considering the enormity of the crimes and the lack of legal experts available, the resulting ability of Rwanda to move past the crimes and onto rebuilding is laudable.

The most remarkable quality of Rwandans rebuilding their country is their focus on reconciliation and forgiveness as the path to peace. A prominent plaque at the entrance of the Rwanda Genocide Memorial sums up the quality cherished above all others in the Rwandan quest for peace, reconciliation, and rebuilding: the quality of Ubumuntu. The plaque reads:

Ubumuntu means humanity-goodness, generosity, and kindness.

"A person who has Ubumuntu is someone who has greatness of heart. In the context of the genocide against the Tutsi, Ubumuntu refers to those who selflessly risked their lives to rescue or help those who were persecuted. We can all be champions of humanity by standing against division wherever we live."

How do you forgive? On our first trip, I was given a chance to ask this question to Pastor Maurice, the director of trauma healing and reconciliation at St. Stephan's cathedral in Kigali. He survived the genocide by hiding among dead bodies and described the horrible sights and smells of those bodies and the memories that plagued him for years. His philosophy focused on the eternal and looked at the big picture. He referred to the genocide as a "dark period" and the successful efforts of rebuilding and developing the country as "changing the darkness into light." He replaced his lost family with his church family. "I now have new families, new smells, and new songs."

According to Pastor Maurice, "We believe that people who do bad things are not themselves in the right place. They are influenced by some dark power... we want people to go against (the darkness)...and forgive. If we don't forgive and go for revenge, we will never have peace, and our children will never have peace. We want to encourage people to forgive as a sacrifice and a seed to build sustainable peace. Forgiveness is the secret for peace in our hearts and the price to build peace in our country and our families for the better future of our children."

Today in the US, we are split in many areas, including politics and values. One of the most significant components of love is acceptance. We are quick to demonize those who believe differently rather than discuss the pros and cons of the issues that divide us. Why not focus on our common beliefs and accept that others may not agree? This does not prevent us from speaking out, but let's focus on the issues themselves and stop demonizing the people. I am particularly sensitive about this issue because I know from my friends in Rwanda that the beginning of the genocide was not the killing; it was the demonization of the Tutsi people. Senior Pastor Sam explains his path to acceptance and forgiveness: "Forgiveness is something God gives you like a heart transplant. I was bitter, I hated, and I felt that I could kill somebody, but God renews you and takes out that bitterness. Bitterness is full-time. You are either bitter forever, or you are free and loving forever. Even if you forgive, it is by God's grace. It was an eight-year journey for me. It's like the scientific process of metamorphosis. You go from a scary caterpillar, ugly, gluttonous, eating all day, and you become a beautiful butterfly, taking nectar, and is loved by kids. I think that is what God is doing for us, and we are not going back to being caterpillars."

I went to Rwanda to find out how to have joy in my life again, but I learned much more. If the Rwandans can forgive, reconcile, and rearrange their families with those that remain after such horrible atrocities occurred in their country, why can't we forgive and reconcile with those family members or coworkers or friends who we struggle with? As Pastor Sam said, 'why are we stubbornly remaining as caterpillars when the free-flying life as a butterfly is within our reach?' One of the best legacies you can leave someone is your example as a peacemaker. Is there someone in your life you are struggling to forgive? Just do it and see how much your life improves. By the way, they don't have to ask for forgiveness to be forgiven, and they might not even accept your forgiveness. Don't let anyone steal the joy rightfully yours; forgive them anyway. The workbook (Part Three of this book) contains an entire section on writing reconciliation letters. Check it out!

Resources:

Left to Tell: Discovering God Amidst the Rwandan Holocaust by Imaculee Ilibagiza.

Eric Harms Memorial Libraries through Books for Africa https://www.booksforafrica.org/donate/donate-project/ rwanda/the-eric-james-harms-memorial-library-kim-harms- pam-pappas-stanoch-rwanda.html.

https://www.redrocksrwanda.com.

The Legacy of Art

Happy are the painters, for they shall not be lonely. Light and color, peace and hope, will keep them company to the end of the day."
—Winston Churchill

Art can serve as a legacy in many ways. The Mona Lisa has inspired people for over five hundred years, as have Leonardo da Vinci's other design endeavors (for example, a prototype for the modern helicopter). Leonardo's contemporary, Michelangelo, also left long-lasting art legacies; such as the statue of David and the Sistine Chapel. The Pieta (which depicts the body of Jesus on the lap of his mother Mary after the Crucifixion) ministered to me after the loss of my own son over 500 years after it was sculpted. In these cases, the art itself lives beyond the life of the artist. It is tangible and gives as much to us in the 2020s as it did to viewers in the 1520s.

But a legacy of art can take many forms. Music, poetry, theater, literature, architecture, dance, and visual arts all live on (if recorded) beyond the artist's life. An introduction to art is another legacy I will refer to frequently.

After my son's death and the loss of my clinical dental career, I was blessed to have an artistic friend who introduced me to a new hobby, porcelain painting! Susan Peterson is a fantastic porcelain painter and offered to give me lessons. I said *yes*! Porcelain painting is considered by many to be a dying art in the US. It was very popular twenty-thirty years ago, and therefore most of the painters are Perennials (this is a new term I just discovered to refer to older adults; a nod to millennials). At my first meeting of the local Porcelain Artists Guild, we celebrated the birthday of a ninety-year-old painter. This was my kind of club!

Learning an artistic skill can be very therapeutic. Once I got the hang of painting and had taken a lot of lessons, I found myself getting lost in my projects. I was having fun. Later I found another artistic legacy leaver, Ione Roland. Ione focused on working with clay. She felt that hand-building clay vases or other pieces brought her closer to nature as clay was from the earth. Ione was eighty-four when I started working with her. She had been widowed years before and lived alone in a little house in the small town of Mayer, Minnesota. She transformed her garage into an art studio. Ione never considered herself alone. "I have my art," she used to say. One day I came over for a lesson and found a life-size statue of Jesus on her table. She had discovered it in a church with its hands damaged and brought it home to fix it. That was Ione; she could fix just about anything with clay!

Porcelain painting filled a void for me. It came at a time when the rest of my life seemed out of control. It was forgiving as everything is reversible until the piece is fired in the kiln. My hands did not always work properly, so being able to wipe the paint away and wait until I had everything done to my satisfaction was a big bonus. It also taught me to look at the world differently. I started looking at colors in a sunset-not just the obvious yellows and blues, but the pinks and magentas, oranges and greys. I became fascinated with trees, the variety of shapes, leaves, and branches, shadows, and colors. Sometimes I would get so caught up in a painting that I would forget the time. Getting lost in my work happened a lot!

We have several art legacy leavers throughout our family. My sister-in-law, Sonja, was a trained visual artist and teacher. She also was a meticulous seamstress. Sonja, inspired by the design of an apron used by her aunt, sewed "Aunt Bessie Aprons." As she made them, she handed them to her siblings (and siblings-in-law.) Each of us has at least one of these precious legacies, and I am carefully preserving mine to hand down to my daughters. We think of Sonja and Aunt Bessie every time we wear them. Former brother-in-law, Danny, wrote songs for his kids. Sue's beautiful soprano voice has been genetically passed down, and this trait shows up frequently in the nieces and even grand-nieces. My niece Heidi is an art teacher and adventurer.

Many of my friends, most of whom had busy careers, are finding that art has improved the quality of their retirement. Sheryl and her husband, Lee, both write poetry. Sheryl composes poems to celebrate weddings, birthdays, and other big events. This serves as stand-alone art and as a historical, literary memento. Lee, who has developed a beautiful collection of arrowheads that he has found throughout the upper Midwest, also writes poetry. He composes them in his head at night and then writes them down as soon as he wakes up. Poetry is particularly helpful in expressing a cognitive awareness of experiences as life changes. Lee and Sheryl leave a remarkable legacy of documentation of significant events and a personal narrative that will be a treasure to their family and friends. Judy writes books, Theresa plays the harp, Carol paints, Pam promotes everything French, Char is an interior designer, and Annie works with stained glass.

I am grateful to Susan and Ione for teaching me new artistic skills. I would like to pass on the secrets of porcelain painting to my grandchildren. Having a hobby gives you something to do when you are finished working. You never have to feel alone!

The dynamic duo of Wendy Short Hays and Elliott Hays have taught theater at Visitation School and St. Thomas Academy for over thirty years. Wendy is the theater director, and Elliott is the technical director. When Eric was a freshman, he had a difficult choice to make. In eighth grade, he had a terrific football season, but he had also been given the role of the king in *The King and I* for the eighth-grade musical. He was great. Eric was already over six feet tall and had an imposing presence. The boys at St. Thomas Academy took turns shaving his head for a fundraiser. The following fall, Wendy asked Eric to try out for the high school fall play, but it would interfere with his football career. Eric loved football, and Eric loved theater. He chose theater, and except for ninth-grade basketball, never looked back on sports. Eric decided to revel in his role as a band and theater geek leader. Wendy and Elliott, and Mrs. Nedermeyer (his band director) became like second parents to Eric. He was blessed, indeed!

Wendy can trace her interest in theater back to her parents. Stories of her dad, "Big Al" Short, became a loving memory to her theater kids. Big Al acted at The Goodman Theater in Chicago for a time before becoming a businessman. Wendy's mom, Louise Edwards, was involved in radio in Indianapolis. She wanted to do a radio talk show and asked her employer to sponsor her idea, or she would quit. Louise got her talk show. Her first interview was with one of the Dorsey brothers. She interviewed a number of celebrities of the time, including Benny Goodman, Hoagy Carmichael, and Laurel and Hardy.

Louise and Big Al supported their daughter as she pursued theater in high school and college. They traveled and sought theater out wherever they could. They attended the original performances of *The King and I*, *My Fair Lady*, and *Hello Dolly*. "I remember my father giving me my first acting note," Wendy remembers. He told me, "Don't drop the ends of your sentences. Keep the energy!"

Wendy attended Southern Methodist University in Dallas and received a degree in Dance and Theater. Her parents were retired, so she decided to come to Minneapolis to visit her brother, and she stayed. Wendy discovered that "Minneapolis is a wonderful place for theater. It is not only a great place to live, it has viable, regional, nationally acclaimed theater programs."

A few years later, Wendy married Elliott Hays, a man of many talents in theater and beyond. He was a divorced father of two, and Wendy embraced her new family. Wendy and Elliott went on to have two children of their own.

In the early 1990s, Wendy and Elliott were doing a show in River Falls, Wisconsin, and a representative from Visitation High School asked her to direct their next musical, *Guys and Dolls*. Wendy took the job and, after a couple of years, came on full-time as the theater director. Not long after, Elliott was hired on as the technical director of theater. And the rest is history. Elliott and Wendy have influenced well over 2500 students in their one hundred productions. In his short time at Columbia, Eric participated in theater with the students at Barnard College and used his oratory skills to be elected to student government. Other students of Wendy and Elliott became professional costumers, professional actors, professional lighting designers, and professional sound designers. Wendy also points out the advantages her students found pursuing professions such as law, business, and design. "We teach our students how to speak and project and present themselves to an audience. These are skills that are useful in many professions." In true legacy-leaving form, several of the Hays children and grandchildren are still actively enjoying participating in theater. The legacy continues!

Thank you, Wendy and Elliott, for enriching my son's life and equally enriching all you touch. You have used your art to weave your legacy into the lives of thousands. Your parents would be so proud of you!

Do you have a hobby or artistic avocation you can pass on to the next generation? Do you have an interest in learning a new one? Can you support someone close to you in their artistic projects? The legacy of art can be represented by the works of art you leave behind or by the encouragement of artistic endeavors in others. Either way, the world gets richer!

Resources:

https://www.joanmitchellfoundation.org/journal/an-artists-legacy
-how-do-you-want-to-be-remembered.

The Legacy of Leonardo: Painters in Lombardy by Bora, Giulio et al. & David Alan Brown; Marco Carminati [ed.].

The Legacy of Trust

The single uniqueness of the greatest leaders
and organizations of all time, is trust.
—David Horsager

My husband Jim described his time growing up on the farm in Blooming Prairie, Minnesota, as one in which, "Your word was your bond." No one locked their doors, children walked to school alone and stayed out until suppertime, and ten-year-olds were expected to drive tractors. That last tractor-driving part was not such a good idea. Jim described an adventure as a young boy involving a tractor, not knowing where the brake was, and a tree. The tree lost in that escapade, and fortunately, Jim was unhurt. His dad had to pay for the tree, though.

Recently, it seems that telling the truth isn't as important as it once was. This is especially apparent when you look at a typical reality television show. What has happened to us?

Regarding relationships, trust is the glue that holds us together. Trust is essential to marriage, family relationships, friendships, and work teams. A lack of trust may keep you from developing close personal relationships. Dependability, reliability, and honesty are essential elements of the work environment. Being trustworthy and learning to trust others increases our ability to function effectively in our personal and professional lives.

I had the privilege of knowing fellow Minnesotan David Horsager, who wrote my favorite professional management book, *The Trust Edge*. I give seminars to dentists on how to manage anxiety and conflict in their offices and recommend his book every time. As the coordinator of Peer Review for the Minnesota Dental Association, I worked with patients unhappy with their dental care. The most important characteristic and theme in both jobs is the building up of trust. The best part of David's book is that he breaks trust down into eight pillars: clarity, compassion, character, competency, commitment, connections, contribution, and consistency. *The Trust Edge* dissects the perplexing topic of trust into concrete concepts that are easy to understand.

Mr. Horsager credits his parents for his interest in trust. I remember David saying that instead of telling him to "have fun" when he left the house, his parents would say, "be good." With that, David was reminded, even as a child, that character mattered, and he needed to be mindful of it at all times. I wonder how different our society would be if we focused less on having fun and more on being good. Of course, being good while having fun is the best combination.

I asked David about the legacy his parents left him. He listed them as character, work ethic, commitment, community, faith, and health. His dad, Clarence, demonstrated integrity by doing the right thing even when no one was looking, consistently. David got to observe this repeatedly, even when Clarence had to deal with difficult people who were not acting with character.

Growing up on a farm, David had to work at an early age, without question. When harvest season came around, his father would shout, "Rise and shine" at 6:00 a.m., and he and his brothers and sisters cooperated. Hard work was just expected, and his dad tried to make it fun. Commitment was important.

When you start something, you finish it. The Horsager kids were taught to do what is right and not just what was easy.

Community was also important. Going to church and serving at church was obligatory. The Horsagers served on volunteer committees in school as well. Their legacy of faith was also important. It wasn't just going to church; it was living the values.

Another significant legacy left by David's parents was a focus on health. His dad is ninety-three, and he and his mom, Mary, still run the farm. They cut down a bit on the acreage, but they still work hard every day, and they live healthily. Clarence and Mary are not legalists, but they believe in moderation. They watch what they eat. They don't smoke or drink. They walk four-plus miles a day.

David also credits his father with helping him to learn the importance of sharing vision, which is a big part of building trust. Clarence had a natural gift of vision sharing.

One of the legacies that Mary left was her involvement in 4-H. As a former 4-H member, I know how much commitment it takes to lead young people in these groups. She was particularly a leader in the area of speech. Mary encouraged her children to participate in the speech programs, and David became the state champion. That championship allowed him to visit Israel and stay with the prime minister's press secretary. Way to go, Mary and David!

David would like to leave the legacies of trusting God and being trusting to his children. "Love God and Love People" describes his faith. He would also like to pass on the value of physical health and relationships.

He is so proud of his wife, Lisa, and his children as he sees them in leadership positions at camps and in his church. He feels blessed that his family gets along and still loves gathering for the holidays. He would like them to grow up kind and courageous.

David's interesting point about trust is that some people lead with trust, and others lead with skepticism. He is quick to point out that neither is better than the other. Those who lead with trust were frequently raised in a trusting environment, and those who lead with skepticism were not. This was an "aha" moment for me. My husband Jim was raised in an environment similar to David's. I was not. Jim was definitely more trusting. Frequently I would get frustrated when he trusted people who were clearly not deserving. He was often hurt and taken advantage of because he could not imagine anyone would lie or cheat him because he would never do that to another person. On the other hand, I approach things with skepticism, and people have to earn my trust. Our marriage was successful for so many years because we accepted our differences. I had a lot more fun because I married Jim, and he avoided a lot of scammers because of me!

If the Harvard study tells us that happiness is dependent on close relationships,[12] and close relationships are dependent upon trust, then trust is a necessary component to improve happiness. By showing your loved ones that you are reliable, honest, and consistent, you build up relationships with them and teach them to be trustworthy by example. Teaching those you care about to embrace the value of trust will lead to enhanced personal and workplace relationships.

Resources:
The Trust Edge by David Horsager.
https://positivepsychology.com/build-trust/.
https://www.betterup.com/blog/how-to-build-trust.

---

[12] https://www.cnbc.com/2023/02/10/85-year-harvard-study-found-the-secret-to-a-long-happy-and-successful-life.html.

The Legacy of Education

*Education, then, beyond all other divides of human
origin, is a great equalizer of conditions of men–
the balance wheel of the social machinery.*
—Horace Mann (1848, as cited in
Education and Social Inequity, n.d.)

My favorite teacher was Miss Sandy Ghettings. She was my senior-
year English teacher in high school. Miss Ghettings made me
feel special. She encouraged me to express myself. She shared
her love of reading with me. Most importantly, she gave me
self-confidence in writing, which, since I took only one semester
of English in college, had to sustain me for life. (Sadly, my eighteen-year-old brain told me to focus only on the sciences. My
sixty-six-year-old brain would have known the value of choosing
more variety in my coursework!)

Teachers are uniquely positioned to help their students
advance in their area of study, cultivate competence, and recognize their talents. When combined with a kind and caring heart,
every teacher has big-time legacy potential!

Nelson Mandela said, "Education is the most powerful weapon
you can use to change the world."[13] This statement is true not only
in Africa but around the world. Many cultures, particularly those

---

[13] futureafrica.science.

facing hardships, recognize this. My Jewish friends described that value passed down from their ancestors as necessary because, "It can never be taken away from you." My husband Jim's father, himself an immigrant, passed the value of education on to his children and served as chair of the local school board.

My childhood instilled in me that I would need to get a good education if I were ever to make anything of myself. Mom taught me that my finger deficit did not limit my future and that I could do whatever I wanted. My father, by continually reminding me that the government required him to take financial care of me only until I was eighteen, taught me that if I wanted to go to college, I better start working hard at sixteen to earn the tuition.

When my children came along, our first investment was in their education. I advised my children to go as far as they could in their field of choice so that they could support their families by themselves if necessary. Both girls had the great fortune of taking a break from their careers while their children were young and starting up their own businesses when the youngest started school.

Unfortunately, access to education around the world is not universally offered, especially among girls and minority groups.

The World Bank reported in 2015 that, "the majority of students in primary and secondary schools in Sub-Saharan Africa still lack the benefit of access to textbooks, and the key reason for this shortage is affordability: textbooks are much more costly in Sub-Saharan Africa than in other developing regions."[14]

Books for Africa founder, Tom Warth, is working on that problem.

Tom was born in England and came to America when he was twenty-four. He settled in Minneapolis, intending to become his own boss. That dream came true when he developed a successful

---

[14] https://openknowledge.worldbank.org/handle/10986/21876.

mail-order book-selling company that specialized in books about classic cars. At first, he bought books and exported them to retailers. Then he began his own publishing company, eventually becoming the largest publisher of classic motor books. Tom was a traveler, and while visiting Jinja, Uganda, a friend showed Tom a local library. Tom was appalled to find very few books in that library, a discovery that led to the founding of Books for Africa, the largest shipper of donated books to the African continent. At this writing, Books for Africa has shipped over fifty-five million books and tablets, in English, French, and national languages, to all fifty-five countries on the continent. Tom's goal is to end the African book famine and have books available to every child.

In many African countries, the availability of information in books or through electronics is limited at this time. Through my work with Tom Warth's Books for Africa, and the establishment of Eric Harms Memorial Libraries, I was able to meet firsthand local heroes who helped those who may not otherwise have access to an education receive one. Like in the United States, educational legacy heroes are simple people with big hearts. I know many educational legacy heroes in Rwanda!

I met Patrice Dorrall when she was serving as the headmistress of White Dove Global Academy in Kigali. Patrice is from the US but is frequently mistaken for Rwandan. Not only has she helped students in her school move ahead in technology and start careers locally, but she has also placed students from her school in some of the best colleges worldwide. She has served Books for Africa in the critical role of shipment coordinator in Rwanda and has helped us connect with many schools and programs needing books. The Eric James Harms Memorial Libraries could not grow without her help.

Clare Effong, a diminutive Nigerian, left her prestigious job in the US to help Rwandans after the genocide. She found a little boy and his sister living in the garbage dump near Kigali and adopted them. That little boy, her adopted son, Justice, eventually graduated from Harvard. Through good times and bad, Clare worked tirelessly, and over many years, to help lift Rwandans up from poverty through education. Her current project, Esther's Aid, is, "Dedicated to inspiring hope by providing free life-changing skills and educational programs to impoverished youth and exploited women."[15]

Clare recognized that workers trained in culinary arts would be needed as Rwanda developed. She started a small school to train them. Within a few years, Esther's Aid became well-known within the hotel community as a place that focused not only on culinary skills but on building character and the positive attitude necessary to learn even more. One of my favorite "Rwandan Moments" was taking Claire out to lunch after visiting her school and being mobbed by the culinary workers at the Marriott as they rushed in to thank "Mama Claire." She is a rock star in Rwandan culinary circles.

Tom Allen is an American working through Bridge to Rwanda who helps promising Rwandan students (like Justice) find amazing educational opportunities. He also, with Dan Klinck and Journeymen International, helped the remote village of Sunzu build a community library and community center. I saw the center transform from an unfinished building to a dynamic library full of activity with its own computer club.

Clare, Tom, and Patrice answered a calling to serve those unknown to them halfway across the globe and are now doing extraordinary things in Rwanda. They are joined by thousands of native Rwandans who make similar sacrifices to help improve educational opportunities for their native countrymen and women.

---

[15] esthersaid.org.

One example of a recipient of a family legacy promoting education is Denyse Mugabekazi. She is now passing that legacy on through her organization Grown to Help, which mentors marginalized families and helps them pass on the gift of education to their children. This is her story in her words. It is repeated thousands of times by parents who work hard and sacrifice to give their children a better life.

WHO AM I, MY STORY, AND MY CAUSE
"My name is Mugabekazi Denyse, I was born in Rwanda, Kigali City, Gitega Sector, one of the most dangerous areas in the city. I grew up in a family of five children. How happy and ambitious a family it was until 1994!

"My father was a journalist in charge of tourism and the environment. My mother worked in the Ministry of Youth, as the secretary and cashier in the Youth Hub in the Kimisagara Sector.

"On January 11th, 1994, early in the morning (it was around 4:00 a.m.), I heard my mother's voice telling us to wake up because our father had just died. He had been killed by the army because he was against discrimination and racism.

"Two months after the genocide against the Tutsi started, we were still grieving for our beloved father, especially my mother. I was a young girl who felt that pain so deeply, but from that day on, I noticed that things had changed, and nothing was going well.

"My mother managed to rescue us from Kigali and take us to the Southern Province, formerly Gitarama, where my father came from. We went to live with our uncle (my father's brother), who protected us until the genocide's end."

Denyse credits her mom with keeping them alive during the genocide and protecting them from witnessing the brutality.

"My mother was always with us, making sure that

if we die, we die together, none could go outside the
house, she was always watching. Glory be to God
for this grace granted to me and my family.
"In 1995, my mother started teaching street children who were
beneficiaries of the Youth Hub, but she was earning very little.
My two brothers were in secondary school, my young sister and I
were in primary school, and the last born was in nursery school.
My mother had to feed us, dress us, watch over us, educate
us, and pay school fees for us; everything was on her head."

Eventually Denyse's mother got a diploma certificate, which allowed her to teach in the primary school, but it paid very little.

"My brothers got a chance to study in Catholic schools. Those
kinds of schools charge less school fees and offer good quality
education, which enabled them to perform well and succeed
easily. One is a priest who lives in France, another one is
a medical doctor, a specialist in research and laboratory,
He works in Namibia. The last biological brother got a
scholarship in the US. He now has a PhD in Electrical and
Computer Engineering from Arizona State University. We
also have a cousin brother who came to live with us when
he was ten. He has a bachelor's degree in construction.
"My sister and I didn't have a chance to study in good schools.
Given my mother's financial capabilities, we would wait for
the government to transfer us to any public school. However,
it didn't stop us from studying with purpose as our mother
always encouraged us to work hard, in order to get good marks.
She used to insist on taking education as the only heritage
she could offer to us. My sister is happily married with two
kids, and here I am with my big dream to help children and
families who might be facing the same challenges as ours."

Her mother convinced Denyse to pursue nursing because of the availability of jobs. Denyse worked in a pharmacy and saved her money for two years then went on to get a bachelor's degree in Rural Development.

"My life at that time was kind of a bad experience, working to get school fees, clothes, shoes, maintaining my beauty as a young lady, and not having any other source of support was one of the hardest experiences in my life. I had no guidance, I had no access to the Internet, I had no laptop. Many times I missed class due to lack of transport fees. The journey was not easy at all. However, I am glad that I made it."

Denyse went on to get a job at Agrotech where she has worked for twelve years. In 2018, she enrolled in a master's program.

"Working with marginalized groups of people dominated my thoughts, and that's when I jumped into the MBA/ Project Management program, with the aim to manage one of the projects concerning community development.
"The knowledge gained there, helped me found Grown To Help, which I started with ten other friends of mine. We share the same passion of empowering vulnerable families, especially children. The name Grown to Help came from my father's name, which means Grow and Help (translated in English), to honor my mother's love for him, her resilience brought so much legacy to our family, which was formed by both of them.
"I don't know where I would have been without my education, my family is now proud of me, and supportive. I really want to help vulnerable women who have a painful background, and who raise their children alone in poverty, so that I can change their lives for the better,

117

*by offering quality education to their children, and
empowering them economically, through GTH programs. "*

GTH does not only help students with a traditional education. They teach their recipients to become economically
self-sufficient by training them in financial literacy and saving
and income-generating activities. Denyse's mother even pitches
in and helps tutor students to increase their academic performance. In the developing world, the struggle to educate children disproportionately affects girls and young women as you
can see reflected in Denyse's own story.

Denyse realized that helping marginalized children thrive in
school requires help in the home. She works with families to assist
them in understanding the importance of education to their children's future. Many parents are so overwhelmed with the challenges of survival today they are unable to grasp the damage done
in the future when they keep their children out of school.

One of her students is Emmanuel Ndayishimiye who is fifteen years old and lives with his widowed grandmother and
three siblings. In order to feed the family, Emmanuel and his
elder brother were told to drop out of school and work.

Once they enrolled in GTH, they were provided with school supplies and book fees, but the grandmother still wanted them to work.

*"My brother and I had to miss school or use hours after class in
the evening or during the weekend to look for manual jobs and
bring money home so that we can eat. "* Emmanuel explains.
Once enrolled in GTH, *"they immediately organized special
mentorship sessions with us and our parents separately. They
have taken us through Children's Rights and Responsibilities.
Our parents learned about positive parenting and their
contribution to their children's academic performance. "*

Emmanuel's grades improved substantially and his grandmother stopped forcing them to work and started encouraging them to study and succeed. According to Emmanuel,

> *"My self-esteem and hope for the future increased. Today I can witness hard-hitting help from GTH. We are no longer kicked out of class due to the lack of school fees or supplies."*

We have numerous educational heroes here in the US as well. One of them is Darlene Miller. Darlene grew up on a Minnesota farm along with seven brothers and sisters. After college, she began working in a tool and die company. After being overlooked and underpaid (she was the only woman working in her position), she bought the company. In 2006, she was the US Chamber of Commerce Small Business Person of the year, and her company, Permac Industries, was the 2008 US Chamber Small Business of the Year and in 2014, Darlene became the first woman President of the Precision Machined Products Association.

Let's face it; Darlene is a big deal! What makes her an even bigger deal in my mind is her support of technical education and that she has worked well with three US presidents representing both parties. One program, Right Skills Now, is an alternative educational program for technology and manufacturing training. Darlene recognized and advocated for technical training (at the national level) for those who were not seeking a traditional college education. A local program offers eighteen weeks of classroom training and a six-week paid internship. It has a 100 percent job placement upon graduation.

My work with Books for Africa has shown me how the educational challenges that poverty brings are universal and that anyone with enough drive and passion can make a difference. Denyse's mother gave that passion and drive to her, and Denyse is passing it down to the students she serves. Darlene has established the need for increased technical education in the US. Claire is making a difference in the hospitality sector, and Tom and Patrice are enhancing lives through the gift of global education. They are heroes in my book, as are all men and women who work to lift their students up and prepare them for life. I am so grateful for the legacy of education I received from the teachers and administrators at St. Hughes Elementary School, Elizabeth Seton High School in Bladensburg, Maryland, and my professors at the University of Maryland, the University of Maryland Dental School, and Loyola University Medical Center.

Resources:
Website: https://growntohelp.org/
Eric James Harms Memorial Libraries through Books for Africa; The Eric James Harms Memorial Library (Kim Harms & Pam Pappas Stanoch) – Rwanda. For more information or to establish a memorial library for your loved one in Rwanda through this organization visit our website https:// www.booksforafrica.org/donate/donate-project/rwanda/the-eric-james-harms-memoriallibrary-kim-harms-pam-pappas-stanoch-rwanda.html or use this QR code:

The Legacy of Faith

*For billions of people, religion is important. The tenants
of a belief system can provide a life's purpose, explain
the surrounding world, and turn death from something
to be feared into a concept that may be comforting."*
—*Jason Boyett, Twelve Major World Religions: The Beliefs,
Rituals, and Traditions of Humanity's Most Influential Faiths*

According to the most recent (2022) Gallup poll, 81 percent of Americans believe in God. It is impossible to thoroughly discuss legacy and death without discussing the importance of faith in shaping our views of both issues. I am a Christian, both feet in, and so most of this chapter will focus on the Christian faith. For those who are not Christian, please interpret God as you see God. For those who do not believe in a higher power, please view this chapter as an opportunity to understand better those who do.

First of all, let me explain my faith. Faith is personal. It is between God and me. The guiding principles are the two most important commandments left by Jesus. They are (rephrased):

Love God with your whole heart, mind, and soul.

Love your neighbor too. (Everyone is our neighbor.)

Although this may seem a simplistic interpretation, I believe it covers everything. If you love God and you love people and act accordingly, it is hard to go wrong.

My first great teacher was my mother. She loved God with her whole heart, mind, and soul. Like the rest of us, she made big mistakes, especially when her mental illness flared up. Despite her challenges, her love of God enabled her to love her children. Mom taught us never to doubt God's love and never to doubt her love for us. We didn't.

One of the challenges of our Christian faith is that we are very clearly instructed to forgive others as God forgave us. Ouch! That is hard sometimes but astonishingly freeing. By taking the unhealthy emotions-the anger, hostility, and desire for retribution-out of our hearts, we can fill it with healthy doses of love, peace, and joy. Forgiveness is part of God's recipe for a healthy soul.

Later on in this book, we will discuss legacy letters. One of the most beautiful I have ever seen was written by my son Eric as a school project. He was instructed to write a letter to someone other than his parents, who had shaped his life, and to tell them how grateful he was for them. His letter to his Aunt Sally makes my heart sing.

To My Dearest Aunt Sally,
In my fifteen years of life, very few things have caused
me more excitement than hearing that my relatives from
Oklahoma were coming for a family holiday. It gives me
great joy to be around my beloved kin, and although our
times together are short, I have learned a lot as a growing
Christian about how to be a loving spouse and parent.
I learned patience as you waited for your
family to get ready for an outing.
I learned respect as you kindly reminded me of
a breach of decorum at family events.
I learned humor when I could hear laughter from
your games of Rook from anywhere in the house.

*I learned thoughtfulness when we were
together on the Germany trip.
I learned hard work when you gladly helped cleanup
on both Christmas and Thanksgiving.
I learned simplicity when you take joy
from the simple pleasures of life.
I learned love when you made a point to say you
loved me when we were at the airport in France.
I learned optimism when I see you almost
perpetually in a state of happiness.
I learned God's joy when I would be looking for
you and track you by following the laughter.
I learned true strength when you try to make it to as many
family gatherings as possible, no matter how long the drive.
How can I thank you enough for the great times you
and your family have provided me over the years? There
are very few words that describe the positive effect you
have had in my life, Sally. Although I have very few
chances of saying it, I love you and always will.
Every time I think of you, I give thanks to my God. And
I am certain that "God who began the good work within
you, will continue his work until it is finally finished on
the day when Christ Jesus comes." Philippians 1:3,5
Your favorite (I hope) nephew,
Eric*

Sally continues her legacy to her forty-plus nieces and nephews. She brightens up any room with her presence.

My husband, Jim's family, was raised Baptist and the conversation he had with his mother Inez about his decision to marry me went something like this:

Jim: *Mom, I am getting married next summer.*

Mom Harms: *Oh, that's wonderful! Is she Baptist?*
Jim: *No, Mom, she is Catholic.*
Mom Harms: *Catholic! Do you have to get married in a Catholic church?*
Jim: *No, Mom, we are getting married in a Methodist church.*
Mom Harms: *Methodist! What's wrong with Baptist?*

For me, the religious denomination is not important. The Catholics, Baptists, and Methodists all believe that the two most important commandments are to love God and love people. There are a few things that I disagree with in all denominations, but as long as they focus on love God and love people, I am okay, as my faith is between God and me. Jim and I thought the important thing for us was that we went to church as a family. We started out in a Presbyterian church, spent some time as Methodists, and settled on Baptist when we moved to Minnesota. Jim's mom was happy!

In true legacy form, Inez passed her faith down not only to my generation but to my children. Eric was Inez's fortieth grandchild. She was eight when he was born and, due to a stroke, spent the years Eric could remember finding it difficult to talk. She showed her love for Eric by running her fingers through his very curly hair. She once told us that she wanted to live long enough to see Eric graduate from high school. She measured her life through her children and grandchildren. Eric wrote another story when he was a sophomore in high school (thank you, Mr. Weber, for assigning these projects) titled, "The Love of God in the Strength of Inez." Eric wrote:

> *"My grandmother Inez was a strong woman, both physically and in character. She was a woman of average size, about five foot six inches with an average build. But she had the spiritual strength of a giant. Grandma had a kind*

*face, brown hair, and an infectious smile. When she
was a young woman, Inez labored in the barn, while her
sisters did the housework. This could account for her great
physical stamina. She was a kind and Godly woman."*

In describing his visits to the nursing home in the last year of
her life, Eric wrote:

*"The simple whit of the room with my grandmother's
personal touches remain to this day my most vivid
memory of her. The decor usually included changing
rounds of family pictures, Christmas cards, and the solid
rock on which she entrusted her salvation, a framed
copy of her favorite hymn, "'Blessed Assurance.'"*

Eric then described his last visit to his grandmother before
she died. (The family frequently gathered around her bed and
sang her favorite hymns.)

*"This traditional hymn ('Blessed Assurance') was the sound
from which I could draw the definition of my grandmother's
creed; "Blessed Assurance, Jesus is mine." It was (one of) the
last song(s) she ever heard, our benediction as our matriarch
prepared for the next life. As I left my beloved grandmother
to sleep, she took upon a familiar gesture of hers, filing her
fingers through my curly hair. It had been done many times
before, but as I felt the aged hand feeling my scalp, the love
of God seemed to pour into me; never before and never to this
day have I felt such a strong love from such a distant body."*

I hope that my grandchildren can say similar things about
me when I am gone!

Faith is frequently passed down through families, both our biological families and "faith families."

Over thirty years ago, a new pastor started at our church, Berean Baptist, in Burnsville, MN. Roger and Joanne Thompson played a big role in my faith life. Joanne ministered to me on numerous occasions and gave great parenting advice. They have always described our church as a "family." They worked hard to create a family atmosphere. During difficult times in our lives, that family played a big role. I watched their faithfulness as Roger led our church through rough times. Writing this book gave me the wonderful opportunity to interview Roger and Joanne to help me understand the faith legacy given to them.

Roger described his father as "incarnating a spirit of servitude and kindness...and he would clean up too." Roger's father wrote his legacy by living well. He was gentle, patient, non-judgmental, and not critical. He embraced a phrase borrowed from Kierkegaard, "Love chooses to understand." Roger's parents were in a serious car accident in 1979. Roger's mother died; she was only fifty-six. Roger's father survived the accident but never displayed any bitterness about the hand life dealt to him.

Roger and Joanne are careful to understand that many do not grow up with a safe life and are careful about telling their family history. Roger points out that he was just one generation removed from an unsafe environment, as his grandfather was an alcoholic. His story shows that when one person changes, generations change.

Joanne feels that, "Everything I do is fueled by the Creator. I hope and pray to draw others into the joy of the Lord. I want my grandchildren to be the unique creations God made them. My legacy is a sense of delivering to them the understanding that God sees you, knows you, and loves you. I want them to know as a reality, not just a religious legacy, but to discover the joy of our salvation. Life is hard, and this world is dark, but God's story is about the joy of his salvation. Jesus is not an idea. Jesus is everlasting, worthy of their pursuit, and He who brings joy."

Mother Teresa had a business card. On one side of the card said, "God Bless You," and had her signature. The other side of the card had a small poem: "The fruit of silence is prayer; the fruit of prayer is faith; the fruit of faith is love; the fruit of love is service; the fruit of service is peace."[16]

I have been lucky. The people who have left me the legacy of faith and given me a secure sense of place in the universe have been honorable, loving people. Unfortunately, in every religion, those with large egos have used hubris (considered the worst of the seven deadly sins) to abuse and betray those looking to find faith. For those of you who believe in a higher power, I hope that belief gives you as much peace as it does me. For those who do not believe in a higher power, perhaps you can look at faith from a *Psychology Today* secular perspective. "Faith is an expression of hope for something better. More than a wish, it is closer to a belief, but not quite. A belief is rooted in the mind. Faith is based in the heart."[17]

Resources:

Where There Is Love, There Is God: Her Path to Closer Union with God and Greater Love for Others by Mother Teresa.

Do the Next Right Thing: Wisdom for Your Next Step by Roger Thompson.

Table Life: Savoring the Hospitality of Jesus in Your Home by Joanne Thompson

Twelve Major World Religions: The Beliefs, Rituals and Traditions of Humanities Most Influential Faiths by Jason Boyett.

---

[16] *Where There Is Love, There Is God* by Mother Teresa.

[17] https://www.psychologytoday.com/us/blog/am-i-right/201209/why-faith-is-important.

The Legacy of Friendship

One of the most beautiful qualities of true friendship
is to understand and to be understood.
—*Lucius Annaeus Seneca*

A few years before he died, Jim became highly interested in a long-term study, The Harvard Study of Adult Development, which began in 1938. It was a terrific study, especially as it discovered that happiness is not determined by fame or fortune or the lack of obstacles you face in your life but by the relationships you build. Jim and I decided that, even though he was constantly almost dying and we had faced many obstacles, we were rich in relationships. I think that philosophy played a role in how he faced his final days calmly, contentedly, and with humor. Thank you, Harvard!

"[C]lose personal connections are significant enough that
if we had to take all eighty-five years of the Harvard study
and boil it down to a single principle for living, one life
investment that is supported by similar findings across a
variety of other studies, would be this: Good relationships
keep us healthier and happier. Period. If you want to
make one decision to ensure your health and happiness, it
should be to cultivate warm relationships of all kinds."
—*Robert Waldinger MD and Marc Schulz PhD, The Good Life*

The Good Life starts out by quoting statistics about what millennials thought were their most important goals. Seventy-six percent said that becoming wealthy was their number one goal. Unfortunately, our social media portrays a "good life" that involves perfect bodies, sunny beaches, and lots of money. According to the researchers who looked at eighty-five years of comprehensive data, the real "good life" is much different.

"The good life is joyful... and challenging. Full of love but also pain. And it never strictly happens; it unfolds through time. It includes turmoil, calm, lightness, burdens, struggles, achievements, setbacks, leaps forward, and terrible falls. And, of course, the good life always ends in death."[18]

I have been blessed with good relationships except for that lonely period between separation from my mother at age six and meeting Jim one month after her death at age seventeen. I am still in touch with my childhood friends and have several long-term friendship groups.

Most groups come and go as people's lives change, but one group that has been meeting regularly in my life for over twenty years is my remarkable book club. I love each member, and we have been there for each other through death and new life, sickness and divorce, and all manner of life challenges.

The Book Club was started by Sheryl Ramstad in her condominium in downtown Minneapolis. I will never forget those first meetings and the amazing books we read. Sheryl's intent was to bring together women from all walks of life to foster strong life-long relationships with one another. We chose books as

---

[18] *The Good Life: Lessons from the World's Longest Study of Happiness* by Robert Waldinger MD and Marc Schulz PhD, Simon and Schuster.

a group, with everyone participating based on their lives and experiences. For books written locally, we frequently had the author in attendance. We also brought props to the meeting. At one early meeting, we were reading a book based in Vietnam. The meeting included a bottle of some sort of alcoholic beverage purchased in Vietnam with a cobra coiled inside the bottle. Not only did everyone refuse to have a drink from that bottle, I couldn't even come close to it; I stayed on the other side of the room the entire night. I have a deep-seated fear of snakes, even when preserved in a bottle of alcohol.

Sheryl has a talent for bringing together a diverse group of women. Our current group consists of Sheryl (lawyer, then judge, then doctorate in nursing), Kris (MBA, adventurer and activist), Martha (bank executive and super grandma), Lindsay (former TV journalist and current real estate expert), Carol (television journalist, news director, and general manager), Diane (former marketing executive and our organizer-in-chief), Char (interior decorator extraordinaire), Guy (retired professor and super-nanny to her grandchildren), Annie (retired dentist and stained glass artist), Judy (international speaker, author, and celebrity marketing guru), Kate (retired physician and sage), Pam (globe-hopping cross-cultural trainer, entrepreneur, Greek grandmother and hostess), Darlene (first woman president of the National Tool and Die association, woman of the year (in many ways), and consummate board member), Teresa (public relations whiz and resident harp player) and me.

We have had twenty years of memorable moments together, but one I will never forget was December 8, 2014. We had all met for Carol's retirement party at a local restaurant. My phone rang; my son-in-law called me to say Ashley was in labor and at the hospital in Kansas City. Her due date was three weeks away, and I was planning to come down in a few days to witness the birth of my first grandson, to be named Eric after his uncle. I was so excited but paralyzed at the same time. How was I going to get to Kansas City in time? Darlene got on her phone to look at the airport schedule. Pam called in her frequent flier concierge to find out how quickly I could get a flight. The rest of the group pitched ideas to get me to Kansas City as quickly as possible. I felt as if I was in a scene from my favorite movie, *Steel Magnolias*, surrounded by people who loved me, had been there with me through my son's death, and were rejoicing with me at the birth of my grandson. It turned out that it was too late to catch a flight, so I ran home, got in my car, and started driving down I-35 to Kansas City. Ashley frequently called on my Bluetooth to update me as to her progress, and just before I hit Des Moines in the early morning of December 9, I got the call that my beautiful, healthy grandson Eric was born. It was a beautiful memory, and I was so fortunate to share it with my friends.

The wonderful thing about having long-term friends is that they know who you are and accept you, warts and all! This is especially important as you age. Things start slipping, primarily your memory. True friends are the ones who will tell you if your tags are hanging out of your blouse, your sweater is inside out, your lipstick is smudged, or there is food dangling from your chin. When you forget your words, they'll help you. When the wrong word comes out, they will translate it to the right one without mentioning it. Friends have your back.

I hope the "friendships" I see displayed on social media and reality TV, where jealousy, intrigue, and backstabbing rule the day are not indicative of the next generation. Life is too short for such drama. True friends are loyal and accepting and a life treasure not to be missed.

I also hit the friend jackpot when it comes to encouragement. It seemed like every time I faced a loss, people were there to pick me up. Terri Hands is an encouragement force of nature. Terri is a family therapist who worked with various churches and helped with Stephen Ministries, which provides one-to-one care to hurting people. She had her own practice but decided a few years back to focus on what she believed to be God's plan for her. One of those plans was to help women who have been trafficked. She became the church and community liaison for trafficking justice. Terri also decided to help those who had lost a child and invited me to meet with others who had faced that loss. Our first "Hope Beyond the Grief" meeting introduced me to women who had lost their children through suicide, illness, accidents, and murder. Each of us had a story to tell, and this group gave us a place where we learned that we were not alone.

At about the same time, Terri started working with 5 Stone Media. Five Stone media was started by five-time Emmy Award-winning producer Steve Johnson and businessman Lee Baile-Seiler. Their mission is to tell the world transformational stories of redemption. At the time, they were working on an educational series for church leaders to help them meet the needs of those suffering catastrophic loss. The first part of their series was "The Worst Loss," which focused on losing a child.

Terri introduced Steve to our group, and most of us participated in telling our story of loss on camera for the series. Later, Our Hope Beyond the Grief group worked together to host a seminar for those suffering a loss and now facing the holidays. It was a fantastic event. There is so much suffering out there.

As time passed, four of our group, who had already lost children (including me) became widows. Terri was there to help us through that time as well.

Two days after my husband Jim died, another incredible friend and encourager showed up, Naomi Rhode. Naomi is a legend in the world of speaking, and she served as my speaking coach. After

Jim died, Naomi told me she had felt called to help encourage widows. Naomi was starting a widows' support group, and the first meeting was the following week. She asked me if I would like to join the group. She didn't have to ask twice! Naomi developed weekly devotions, and we met on Zoom. This has been a lifeline for me as an opportunity to share our fears and hopes with others who understand our pain. These women became my dear friends. Every year we have a retreat and meet in person. As of this writing, we are in year three, week twenty-eight of our weekly meetings. We even wrote a book about our group, *Naomi and the Widow's Club: A Safe Strong Place After the Loss of a Spouse.*

The best way to leave a legacy of friendship is to *be* a good friend. Friendships require nurturing. Our book club works because we meet regularly, and we do our best to meet monthly, but sometimes we skip a month. We also support each other, and occasionally meet individually to go to a movie, play, lunch, or breakfast. Sometimes we travel together in small groups.

As we get older, we may find that we get lonelier as friends move away, become debilitated, and even die. Just as we work hard to stay physically healthy, we must keep our connections strong to help us stay emotionally healthy. I am happy to see that my daughters and their husbands make time in their lives for long-term friends. They each have a solid group, many from childhood, and all drama free. I hope my grandchildren are watching their example.

Resources:

Naomi and the Widows Club: A Safe Strong Place After the Loss of a Spouse by Naomi Rhode and Kim Harms. https://www.fivestonemedia.com/.

The Good Life: Lessons from the World's Longest Study of Happiness by Robert Waldinger MD and Marc Schulz PhD, Simon and Schuster.

The Legacy of Shedding (Especially Your Stuff!)

*Can you truthfully say that you treasure something buried so
deeply in a closet or drawer that you have forgotten its existence?
If things had feelings, they would certainly not be happy. Free
them from the prison to which you have relegated them. Help
them leave the deserted aisle to which you have exiled them.*
—Marie Kondo

At a recent wedding of a nephew, I had the happy chance (as I was the only baby boomer on the Harms side of the family who was able to make it to the Mexican resort location) to hang out with the nieces and nephews by the pool and listen to their interesting conversations. One frequent topic of their discussion was the concern that when our generation died out (which was already starting to occur), they would be stuck getting rid of our stuff. At first, I thought the concern was for the older family members. After all, Jim was the twelfth, and I was seven years younger, so they couldn't be talking about me! *But they were!*

I was included in their trepidation. I should have known. When we downsized to a condo, we moved a five-bedroom home into an oversized garage in the Northwoods. Jim and I were somewhat successful at distributing the contents of that garage when Ashley moved into her first home in Kansas City and had no furniture. Jim (I was his passenger) drove a big U-Haul down to Kansas City full of couches, beds, dressers, chairs, and dining room furniture. Seeing our precious belongings appreciated and used by our children felt good.

The garage, however, was still full of "stuff" that neither child wanted. That did not worry me at first as I was sure that someday in the future they would come to their senses and realize the value of all the treasures Jim and I had accumulated in our forty-plus years of marriage. So far, that day has not come.

A few years before Jim passed away, Hillary and her husband, Mike, in as kind and loving a way as possible, told us that we could not die until we cleaned out the garage. All hope of their epiphany that our "stuff" was valuable and worthy of keeping was lost. My dear Jim, in his typical independent way, died anyway, leaving me to pick up the disposal responsibility. I thought I was making good progress as, for two years in a row, I had employed the help of one of my strong great-nephews to clean out the junk, and each year, we filled a dumpster with boxes, water-damaged books, and unused lumber. A carload of books was donated to Books for Africa. I thought that only the good stuff was left. Wrong again!

Let's go back to that poolside in Mexico, listening to the fears expressed by the next generation of my family. I quickly discovered that I was included on the "concern list." It was not up for interpretation as my niece gently asked me if I would like her help to get things "organized."

You see, Jim and I were and are closet hoarders. Our living spaces are well-kept and clean (most of the time), but our closets (and garages) are packed. Like many in our generation, we experienced hard economic times and developed anxiety about letting go of anything that still worked. (Well, to be completely honest, sometimes things were broken, but we held on to them anyway in hopes of getting them fixed; you never know when they will come in handy!) The problem was that, even if these items came in handy, we would not be able to find them, which frequently led to our having multiples. After Jim's death, we found seven chainsaws, some broken, some working. Jim loved to garden and cut down dead or damaged trees. If he couldn't find the tool needed for his next project, he bought another one. I am also guilty of this offense. We would have a lot more in our retirement fund if we were just organized enough to use our possessions wisely. Three months after our poolside discussion in Mexico, I employed my niece Anna to clean out my closets. It was painful, but it was a very wise investment for me. I love going into my closets and finding what I want. I have also instructed my children that they have one year to take whatever they want from the garage, and after that, I am hiring professionals to clean out the garage down to the bare bones of tools and equipment I am currently using.

Hillary suggested that if I buy anything, I must get rid of something else. This is excellent advice and makes me think twice before I buy. The reality is that at my age, I have everything I need.

My cherished friend and fellow widow, Kathy Dempsey, wrote the book on shedding. Really! Her award-winning book *Shed or You're Dead: 31 Unconventional Strategies for Growth and Change* discusses our need to continue to shed whatever is holding us back and allow us to move forward. That includes stuff!

Kathy starts the book with a forward from her sidekick, Lenny the Lizard, and a strong theme in the book is that if a lizard does not shed its skin, it dies. Sometimes, especially as we age, we forget the joys of learning, we stagnate, and we give up. I found that my latest organizational purge has given me a new sense of peace in my home. I also save a lot of time looking for things.

My son-in-law Mike is very organized. He purges through his home regularly. His garage is well ordered, and everything is in its proper place. His mother taught him well in this area.

It is no surprise to me that Mike's sister, Angela, a certified public accountant, keeps people organized and on track both financially and with their personal effects. Her company, Simplify Wealth, helps people in Minnesota manage their finances and households. Her company also provides a personal representative to help people downsize or dispose of property. Angela describes the growing need for our aging population to ensure their estates are properly managed. This will help ensure that their heirs can access what they need at the time of their death. Many of her clients are in their eighties and either have no children or the children live out of town.

Angela describes the paralysis of some of her clients when facing the future. Downsizing or moving into assisted living or a nursing home may seem overwhelming. She describes the importance of family members helping their aged relatives downsize a little at a time and starting early. Angela also recommends an accountability partner to help in the downsizing process.

How do you get rid of belongings you are not currently using? That depends on what your comfort level is and how many people you have to help you. Keep a box somewhere handy in the house for anything you want to give away, and make it a priority to find one thing a day to donate. If you have special items you would like to give to a family member, place them in a special box and review the box each time you meet with family. There are even easy apps available (Thingeology is one example) to help you record the history of your treasured possessions. New and creative apps are developing to help all the time. Some of us may need to ask our grandchildren for assistance with technology and that can create fun memories as a bonus. Throw away outdated things and expired things that no one will use. Do this consistently, and you can make some headway. If you have family members who can help, throw a disposal party and let them know that you are cleaning things out on a certain weekend and would welcome their help. If they are young and just building up their households, you might benefit from seeing your possessions find new homes within the family. In my case, I bartered some items in exchange for cleanup help. It was a win-win for all of us.

Jerry Seinfeld has a great YouTube clip about our relationship with stuff.[19] My favorite part of that clip is his description of personal storage units. Mr. Seinfeld says, "A personal storage unit... is the saddest of all. Instead of free garbage, you pay rent to visit your garbage. It's like a prison visit when you go there." The truth doesn't have to hurt; it can also be funny.

There are many options for unwanted items. You can recycle, sell, donate, or throw away. Fortunately for those of us terrified at the thought of holding a garage or estate sale, professional companies are now available to help us out, and the number getting into this field of work is growing just in time. Check the Internet for a mover, disposal company, or estate sale host near you!

Resources:

Shed or You're Dead by Kathy Dempsey.
https://www.simplify-wealth.com.

https://life-organizer.com
https://gentletransitions.net.

---

[19] https://deadline.com/2014/12/jerry-seinfeld-tonight-show-garbage-video-1201335222/.

https://www.rosesdaughters.com.

https://www.aarp.org/home-family/your-home/info-2021/ simple-decluttering-and-organization-tips.html.

https://www.aarp.org/home-family/your-home/info-2021/ things-to-throw-away.html.

https://www.aarp.org/caregiving/home-care/info-2017/down-sizing-sell-items.html.

Thingeology App

The Legacy of Mentorship

A mentor is someone who sees more talent and ability within you, than you see in yourself, and helps bring it out of you.
—Bob Proctor

My first mentor was my mother. She was loving, caring, and perhaps overly concerned about my lack of fingers (Chapter One: "Your Life Is Your Legacy.") Mom taught me that I could do anything I wanted. She even bought me a piano. Although I left her care before I could become very proficient, her dreams of having a virtuoso, seven-fingered piano player in the family set me up for the possibility of becoming a seven-fingered dentist. Mom taught me to aim high!

Because of the circumstances under which she inherited us (she married a man without knowing he had children and suddenly three children were dropped in her lap while pregnant with her first child), my stepmother Adrienne never accepted the role of mother substitute. As children, we were unaware of the details of that arrangement and could never understand why the unconditional love displayed by my mom had now been replaced with resentment from our stepmother. We were traumatized by this transition. We were brought to Maryland in 1961, and Dad still had his ship command. Once the Cuban Missile Crisis occurred and Dad was called back to the Pentagon for rocket scientist duties, he became resentful too. A house full of resentment is a bad place to raise kids.

Fortunately, in fourth grade, Gene Marie Brown, my second mentor, came into my life. Mrs. Brown was a 4-H leader, and I was lucky to join her group. Mrs. Brown taught me life skills like how to cook, bake, and sew. She took us on outings, laughed with us, cried with us, and cared about us. Mrs. Brown had a wonderful husband (who tolerated our group with great humor) and three children. Sarah was my age and in our group. Although the Brown house was simple, Mrs. Brown made it warm and welcoming, with exquisite aromas emanating from the kitchen. Mrs. Brown's carrot cake became our go-to recipe for special events. I even passed it on to my niece, Sandy, who is a professional caterer, and it became one of our family wedding cake recipes. The vast majority of happy events that I remember from my later childhood involve Mrs. Brown, and her memory stayed with me through adulthood every time I made her carrot cake.

Sadly Mrs. Brown died from cancer in the 1990s. Before she died, we were able to have a Greenbelt Lucky Leaves 4-H reunion, and I shared with her how much she had impacted my life. I was so happy to have that opportunity. Gene Marie Brown, you are one of my heroes!

Even adults need mentors. When I began practicing dentistry in Minnesota, I discovered my female colleagues from the University of Minnesota were blessed with the presence of the legendary Dr. Anna Hempel.

Dr. Hempel was a force of nature and a model of resilience. Dr. Hempel was born in Yugoslavia in 1922. The period between World War I and World War II was one of instability and insecurity, ultimately rising to political extremism leading to World War II. She left Yugoslavia for Tubingen, Germany, with dreams of becoming a dentist. She began her dental training in Germany in

1941 and decided to finish her clinical training at the University of Leipzig. She traveled to Leipzig to locate an apartment. Unbeknownst to Anna, 400 British aircraft were also traveling to Leipzig with over 1400 tons of explosives. Anna awoke from her first night in Leipzig by being blown from her bed. The hotel she was staying in as well as much of the University of Leipzig had been destroyed. When she realized that the dental department would not re-open in Leipzig, she decided to head back home to Yugoslavia. Instead, she got off the train in Vienna and checked out the dental school there. Amazingly, she was able to register and actually complete her studies in Vienna. Unfortunately, during the war, Anna and her fellow students lost their citizenship, their homes were destroyed, and their families were in refugee camps. They were not able to get their dental school credentials due to the political climate and the discrediting of their German training in Tubingen. In 1946, Anna got a job as a dental assistant at the American Air Base in Tullin. Eventually, she returned to Germany to finish her studies at the University of Heidelberg, received her degree in 1947, and her thesis a year later.

A young mechanical engineer, Erwin Hampel, swept her off her feet. They married and decided to come to the US. A Minnesota dentist, Dr. William Neinaber, took her under his wing and eventually convinced her to come to Minnesota to gain the necessary credentials to practice as a dentist. When she arrived in Minnesota, she discovered that she still needed two more years of training to practice dentistry in the state. Anna Hempel was very well educated by the time of her graduation in 1956. The University of Minnesota Dental School recognized this and hired her, originally part-time, then full-time. Eventually, she became a department chair. Anna taught many subjects due to her extensive sixteen-year journey through what she described as the "three best dental schools in the world!"

Anna did not just lead her students clinically. She was a pioneer for women in dentistry. At one point, she was told that a junior professor the university was hiring would be making more than she did as a department head because "he had a family to support." Eventually, in her quiet but persistent way, she contributed to the university's understanding that men and women in the same position deserve the same pay; and she got it. On a daily basis, she was described as informative, encouraging, and uplifting by her former students. Anna held many prestigious positions around the country, some as the first woman. In 1985, she was named the Century Club Professor of the year. I met Anna when she was in her late nineties and was astonished at her history, kindness, and clarity of purpose. Anna passed away at the age of one hundred, having served as a trailblazer, an advocate, and a mentor to thousands of dental students who were trained under her watch.[20]

When my daughter asked me to join her business and in starting my dental speaking career, my mentors showed up—in droves! I reached out to some wonderful people, including Lois Banta and Linda Miles, who encouraged me to write a book, and Vanessa Emerson got my feet off the ground by showing me how to set up a website. Vanessa encouraged me to speak and supported my business 100 percent. Anne Duffy began a program to help women in dentistry and launched an amazing program called DEW: Dental Entrepreneur Woman. She now mentors women nationwide.

Naomi Rhode served as my speaking coach, but her involvement in my life went far beyond coaching. Naomi Rhode "just happened" to be there when I needed help in many ways. Naomi

---

[20] *And That's How It Happened* by Dr. David Born, University of Minnesota, *Dentistry*, Fall/Winter 2019.

(along with Linda and Lois) is one of the dental-speaking world's biggest icons. She was not only president of the National Speakers Association in the US, but she was also president of an international Speakers Association.

Even as adults, we need mentors.

My daughters, Hillary and Ashley, were blessed by numerous mentors along their way. Some were teachers, some were from our church, and some were friends. Sheryl Ramstad, a long-term friend who was an attorney and judge, took them to a legal meeting with her in Chicago where they met prominent attorneys from all over the country. It was at that meeting that both girls started to consider law as a profession. Sheryl continued to support the girls throughout their law school and legal careers.

Our son, Eric, had many wonderful mentors, including teachers and directors. When he was in high school, he created a History Day project around the story of housing discrimination in the 1970s faced by my dental colleague, Dr. Norman Coates, and his wife, Martha. At that time, Martha and Norman were both graduates of prestigious colleges on the East Coast and Norman was attending dental school. As they searched for homes, they discovered that the apartments that were available when they spoke to the landlords on the phone (both have beautiful speaking voices) were suddenly rented when they arrived for the showing, and the same landlords realized that Martha and Norman had some African ancestors. Eric took that project to the state tournament.

The Coates supported Eric by showing up to his plays in high school. Norman shared Eric's interest in jazz music and even took him out to a local jazz club. When Eric was looking at colleges, Norman was able to get Eric an interview at a prestigious university. He also encouraged Eric to study engineering and then law. All three of the Coates' daughters are attorneys.

Children need caring adults in their lives to build resilience and thrive.[21] Norman and Martha took time out of their busy schedules to show an interest in the life of a young high school student in a way that Eric's parents, who had no understanding of jazz music, could not.

A few years back I met, John Turnipseed, a mentor extraordinaire at a 5 Stone Media event. John was a former drug dealer, pimp, and gang leader who transformed into a community leader, pastor, speaker, and served as the Director of The Center for Fathering and Vice President of Urban Ventures, ministering to the same neighborhood he and his crime family used to terrorize. Check out his YouTube Video *Fix the Roof*. In it he tells of his 10 family members convicted of murder and the need for fathers (the roof of the family). John's life was changed by his faith and one mentor who believed in him. John went from drug dealer to hope dealer. John explained in his talk " I want people to understand what a hope dealer is. A hope dealer is someone who gives enough, cares enough about another human being to enter into a stranger's life and offer hope." People can do amazing things if they understand that together we can fix the roof.

You can develop the legacy of mentorship in many ways. You can give hope, (John Turnipseed) help people in their training (Anna Hempel), advise them in life, show them a new path, teach them a new skill, champion a cause, advise them, and tell them the truth (which is sometimes hard). Good mentors are good listeners. Being a mentor can also mean just showing up.

Is there someone in your life who would benefit from your interest in them or your expertise in a specific area? If so, become a mentor!

---

[21] https://info.searchinstitute.org/developmental-relationships-help-young-people-thrive.

Resources:

Dare to Lead by Brené Brown, https://www.audible.com/pd/
    Dare-to-Lead-Audiobook/B07DJYBXNC).

https://en.wikipedia.org/wiki/Mentorship.

Bloodline by John Turnipseed

https://youtu.be/DLnaMO73lsg.

https://www.youtube.com/watch?v=sL3Ntcb50wA.   Fix   the
    Damn Roof! By John Turnipseed at TEDxTC

https://www.fivestonemedia.com/the-turnipseed-trilogy/

https://www.youtube.com/watch?v=LteZuADO780

The Legacy of Family Traditions

Family traditions are more than arguments with the dead, more than collections of family letters you try to decipher. A tradition is also a channel of memory through which fierce and unrequited longings surge, longings that define and shape a whole life.
—*Michael Ignatieff*

One of the best things about Jim's family is that they are rich in family traditions. Most of these traditions revolve around the holidays and involve some sort of food or game or pageant. In fact, the Harms family has a seventy-year-old tradition of hosting a Christmas pageant. We have pictures of Jim as a child participating in the pageant hosted in his family home in Blooming Prairie, Minnesota. The Harms sisters made the costumes. As we had children, each of them would take a role along with their cousins. The smallest baby would be Jesus. If there were two babies, the older one would become Jesus going into Egypt. We would adapt the pageant to the players; sometimes, we even had sheep and, one year, a donkey. The prime role was Mary. Jim, as an adult, frequently served as the narrator. The older kids would help the younger kids costume up. The angels had rosy cheeks painted on, and the shepherds wore beards. The wise men's crowns were sometimes fabulous and sometimes lost and replaced with ones from Burger King.

It was a joyous occasion. The Harms family were singers, and Judy and Sue would lead us as we sang *Silent Night, We Three*

Kings, and *Oh Little Town of Bethlehem.* At the end, we would frequently try to sing something in Norwegian. Our ending was always a hearty rendition of *We Wish You a Merry Christmas* with Uncle Gaylen's untraditional ending of "Lots of candy and *nuts* to you!!!! (Heavy emphasis on the nuts!)

For about twenty years, Christmas Eve and Easter were held at our home in Farmington, and we loved to welcome all the family and friends who visited us. Our Easter tradition included an Easter egg hunt for adults and kids. The Easter eggs had candy or numbers corresponding to a small gift or gift card with a grand prize of $20 egg. We also had an egg toss and egg wars contest. Egg wars involved first decorating an egg as a warrior. Jim would then make up brackets that would pit one cousin, aunt, or uncle against another. The participants would sit on opposite sides of a table covered with newspapers (egg wars is messy) and try to break their opponent's egg. The player with the last egg unbroken was the winner. One of the wonderful things about egg wars was that anyone could win, including small children. The champion would be enthusiastically cheered and photographed wearing the official Harms Egg War Champion Belt.

Unfortunately, COVID broke up our large family celebrations, but we are starting them over in smaller groups.

Family traditions give our children a sense of belonging; they teach shared values, and they bring meaning to celebrations. We come closer together as we celebrate these rituals. Traditions strengthen our bonds as a family.

Not all traditions have to be focused around a holiday. You can start traditions at work or on the first day of school or use them to celebrate a season. Hillary takes the kids to Dairy Queen every Friday after school, and in her family, every Tuesday is Taco Tuesday. She likes to garden, and her children join her. Then in the late summer or early fall, she hosts a canning party.

Ashley's family has traditions surrounding sporting events. The extended family gathers together whenever a big game takes place. Most of these events include a wonderful meal served up by Ashley's Italian mother-in-law, Cathy.

According to the American Psychological Association, "Family routines and rituals are important to the health and well-being of today's families trying to meet the busy demands of juggling work and home, according to a review of the research over the past fifty years. The review finds that family routines and rituals are powerful organizers of family life that offer stability during times of stress and transition."[22]

When I was in school, we didn't celebrate birthdays, so I made sure my family celebrated birthdays. We always had breakfast in bed and a big birthday dinner. My sister-in-law, Sylvia, takes every one of her twenty-two grandchildren out to breakfast. She also makes them an apple pie every fall when they are in college. On New Year's Day, she invites us over for Norwegian meatballs. And, of course, every holiday somehow includes the making of *lefse*, the Norwegian potato version of a tortilla. Birthdays in sister-in-law Judy's family include her famous angel food cake with burnt butter frosting. (See appendix one for the recipe.)

Some family traditions, like a regular family mealtime together, have proven beneficial results. According to Anne Fishel, a family therapist, "I sort of half-joke that I could be out of business if more families had regular family dinners because so many of the things that I try to do in family therapy actually get accomplished by regular dinners. There have been more than twenty years of dozens of studies that document that family dinners are great for the body, the physical health, the brains, and

---

[22] https://www.apa.org/news/press/releases/2002/12/rituals

academic performance, and the spirit or the mental health."[23]

I asked Minal Sampat ("Legacy of Hard Work") if her Hindu family had any special traditions. She replied, "Diwali is the start of the Hindy new year (usually in the Fall), but also the business new year. Every Diwali, we visit our businesses for "Chopda Pujan," which roughly translates to the prayer for books. We get a new book and start our business records for the new year in the book. When I can't be in St. Thomas to celebrate Diwali, my parents Facetime me, and I write my new book for the year as they are writing in their new book!"

Teresa Fong Sit explains, "When my grandparents came to the US, they had a desire to acclimate to the American culture. We didn't formally celebrate any Chinese holidays or traditions. I grew up in a Christian culture with belief in God/Christ rather than Buddhist beliefs or practices.

"The most memorable Chinese custom I grew up with were gifts of money in a red envelope, "lucky money," given by my grandparents, parents, or uncles and aunts for any special day worth celebrating. In my family, most of the adults have a stash of cash and red envelopes around the house, just in case that special child, niece, or nephew comes to visit!"

Ron Hauptman ("Legacy of Resilience") celebrates Passover and a Seder prayer ceremony with his family at his home or his brother's home. He used to celebrate it at his parent's home. "The Last Supper was a seder" Ron reminds me. Getting season tickets to football games was another tradition enjoyed by the Hauptmans.

Last summer we may have started a new tradition in the Harms family. My grandniece, Emma, asked all six of my grandchildren to be in her wedding. Little Eric was the ring bearer

---

[23] https://www.gse.harvard.edu/news/20/04/harvard-edcast-benefit-family-mealtime.

and the five girls were flower girls. At the reception, son-in-law Mike jokingly asked seven-year-old Eric if he had his ring-bearer speech ready. Eric initially panicked but then began furiously writing a speech on his napkin. Not to be outdone by the ring-bearer, the three older girls also wrote speeches on their napkins. Colin, the groom, now in on the joke, announced that it was time for the ring bearer's speech. Eric did a phenomenal job followed by twins, Anna and Lily, all three congratulated the bride and groom and added a personal note. Heidi, age six, although not really sure what a speech was, was determined not to be left out of the limelight. She decided to go with something she was familiar with. "I pledge allegiance to the flag of the United States of America," she began at her turn. Everyone in the room burst into laughter, stood up, and joined her in the Pledge of Allegiance. This was followed by thunderous applause. What began as a joke perpetrated on a seven-year-old, became a definite hit, and the possible genesis of a new tradition of ring bearer and flower girl speeches at family weddings.

This chapter, like this book, focuses on the positive aspects of traditions that lift people up and bring people together. Traditions that limit people in any way or use shame or manipulation to restrain or control them should be changed.

Affirming traditions help us understand our connection to the past. They also connect us with our family and friends. One of the most wonderful things about traditions is that you can always start new ones.

Resources:
https://www.betterup.com/blog/family-traditions
https://www.motherduck.com.au/why-family-traditions-are-so-important-and-how-to-createyour-own/

Part Two:
Death and Dying

Working Towards a Good Death

*We only surrender our body in death–our
heart and soul live on forever.*
—Mother Teresa

It's time! You knew it was coming! I put the word "die" right in the title. Now we are going to talk about death and not about death in general terms. We are going to talk about our own death. Whew, it's out there now, no turning back. We can do this!

One of the things we share is that we are all going to die. Hopefully, not today or tomorrow, but someday.

When I was in high school, I planned for college. In college and dental school, I prepared for my work life. During my work life, I planned for retirement. I am now in that critical interval between menopause and death, where I have no choice but to deal with the first and plan for the second. Let's get to the planning!

Most of the other phases in life come in predictable patterns, but death is different. It can come at any time. So, realistically, we should be preparing our lives to face an unexpected death by building our legacies and minimizing the cleanup of our stuff and our finances. Had I started my legacy binder and legacy thinking a lot earlier, I would not have a garage packed with stuff that no one wants or a box full of completely unorganized financial records. Had I lived my life with a legacy in mind, I probably would have used my resources more wisely.

The fear of death is thanatophobia. This could involve the fear of the dying process or the fear of being dead. Frequently, this death anxiety causes us to avoid facing the inevitable and therefore being ill-prepared when death occurs, or we find out that our death is imminent. Even physicians struggle to tell us that it is likely we will die soon. No physician told us Jim was dying, although it was clearly evident to the home health nurses who recommended hospice. Because of their loving intervention, Jim was able to die the way he wanted.

My hope is that this book will help readers be prepared for their death whenever it might come. I hope it will help save you the strain of a last-minute realization that those they leave behind will suffer grief at not only their loss but also the chaos of unorganized financial records, lack of direction as to the inheritance of property, and confusion as to your wishes concerning the handling of your remains.

If you find yourself feeling overwhelmed because you have not started this process, you are not alone. According to AARP, 60 percent of American adults over eighteen have not even drawn up a will. Fortunately, as we get older, we get better at this, and the majority of baby boomers (58 percent) have at least taken that first step.[24]

Part two of this book focuses on the process of death itself and how we can prepare for it. Of course, the best way we can prepare for long life and extend our death planning time is to exercise, eat wisely, and moderate (or eliminate) any bad habits we have. There are many great health books and resources out there that can help you extend your life or quality of life so that you can build more legacy.

---

[24] https://www.aarp.org/money/investing/info-2017/half-of-adults-do-not-have-wills.html.

But the reality is that no matter how low your cholesterol is, no matter how many push-ups you can do, and no matter how far you can run, death will eventually catch up with you. Everyone needs a plan!

According to the New England Journal of Medicine, 30.7 percent of Americans died at home in 2017, surpassing the number dying in a hospital, 29.8 percent for the first time since the early twentieth century. Deaths in a hospice facility have increased and were up to 8.3 percent in 2017, while nursing home deaths were down to 20.8 percent.

In preparation for this book, I became certified as a death doula (or end of life doula). Death doulas are trained to care for someone at the end of life, to care for them emotionally and spiritually and in a non-judgmental manner. We are not trained to take care of the dying medically. The programs are new and not yet well regulated at this writing, but I suspect they will evolve. The field is fascinating. The ultimate death doula role model was Mother Theresa. She left a comfortable life in Europe to care for the dying poor in India. She once said, "In twenty-five years, we have picked up more than thirty-six thousand people from the streets, and eighteen thousand have died the most beautiful deaths.[25]

One of the main functions of a death doula is active listening so that we can respond better to the wishes of the client and the family. We can help people develop a legacy and life review project, provide respite care, discuss advance care directives, help the family understand and cope with the dying process, and conduct vigils. Sometimes the dying need to have permission from the family to "let go," and doulas can help recognize when this is appropriate. Even those who seem to be unconscious may

---

[25] https://www.quotesgeeks.com/mother-teresa-quotes-on-death/.

be able to hear, so it is important to keep talking to them as if they can hear. End-of-life doulas may also help the family with home organization after and before the death, provide support, or even help after the loss of a pet.

An important question to ask those who are facing their imminent death is how they want to live today. One reason to get your affairs in order today is to allow you to focus on living fully every day you can if you find your death is close at hand.

An end-of-life doula can assist in providing a break for family members. Frequently those in hospice require twenty-four-hour care. Jim was at this point in the last few weeks of his life. Fortunately, we were all set up for hospice. We had a comfortable adjustable bed, a one-floor plan, and easy access to Jim's oxygen machine. I had been emotionally preparing for this for months, so I was ready, and since Jim's decline occurred during COVID, I was very comfortable staying in the condo and ordering groceries. A year before, I would not have thought of those options! If I had to work (there were no speaking jobs available, so I gave webinars), or needed anything, Jim's sisters, the dynamic duo, Judy and Sue, were always there to help. I can't say enough good things about Judy and Sue; they just are there when you need them and, in this case, served the role of uncertified end-of-life doulas.

My favorite death doula role is developing a legacy project. This is a simple process and is described in section three of this book. By helping others write or tell their stories, I learn more about them. I also learn more about their history. An early legacy project that my son Eric and I did while he was in high school was to transcribe and digitize the diary of a World War II tail gunner turned dentist after the war. The description of the primitive planes, the number of his colleagues lost, and the close relationships developed under those difficult circumstances opened our eyes to the sacrifices made by the "greatest generation." One story I will never forget was that he had been injured by some shrapnel and was sent to the hospital. The next day his plane went up without him and was shot down. The entire crew, including his tail gunner substitute, was killed. The grief and guilt he expressed were palpable. Why was he still alive and his crew dead? How could he live with himself knowing that another tail gunner had taken his place? But death is like that. It doesn't always make sense.

My friend, Julie Hull, is a therapist who helps people work through life issues, including death. She has a lot of experience helping others. She was a hospital chaplain and now has her own private practice. Julie's first husband, Ken, passed away from cancer when their son was young. After many years, she found and married another wonderful man, Steve. A few months later, Steve was diagnosed with stage four cancer, and Julie and Steve are now in the midst of a very difficult battle. Despite that, she has given me the wonderful gift of sharing her thoughts on death and legacy.

"I was raised to assume everything is dangerous... just to be safe. It could have been due to my very stoic parents, who loved me and were not equipped to talk about feelings, especially about death. We lost people and people passed; we did not have the vocabulary to say 'died' or that they were 'dead.'
"This dynamic, while still very prevalent in today's culture, caused me to be very fearful of death. As I grew up, I experienced multiple deaths of people who were very close and dearly beloved. With each experience, my acceptance of death and my attitude toward death began to change dramatically. Perhaps this was in preparation for my life's work as a grief specialist and former hospital chaplain.
"I believe everyone has the right to have their own unique

feelings about death. Each one of us has the right to talk about those feelings. One of the most important things I have learned from years of being in the helping profession as a grief counselor is that we can use our beliefs about God or our higher power to help us deal with our feelings of grief, loss, and the very mysterious aspects of death."

"It is inevitable we will all die. In the meantime, I'm very grateful for projects such as this book that allow us to have open conversations about death and legacy.

"It is challenging to find the right words to get the conversation started. When my husband was nearing the end of his life, we would have these death and legacy conversations. We would talk about what he would like to be remembered for and what his end-of-life wishes were. It still strikes me as ironic that we waited so long to have deep conversations about death and the dying process. We didn't have a sense of urgency, and he was in hospice!

"As I look back now, I realize we did not have the vocabulary around the topic. We had the safety and deep love for each other, but we wanted to deny the reality, yet intellectually all the evidence was glaringly real.

"I will leave a legacy of hope. What does that mean exactly? For me, hope is a state of being, a conscious choice to look for inspiration in the dark. In the face of death, whether our own or a loved one, each one of us can consciously choose to give our power to hope or give our power to fear. I found this truth especially powerful in the face of death when I was walking alongside my husband and many loved ones who were nearing death.

"I encourage each one of us to press in to find out the wishes of our loved ones, to start the conversation by simply saying, 'we haven't really talked about how you're feeling right now,'

and 'what are your unique feelings about death? Have you thought about legacy and what that means to you?'

"Regardless of timing, this is such an important conversation to have in order to love well and to 'leave a legacy to die for,' as Kim so poignantly speaks of in the introduction.

"One of my favorite quotes captures my thoughts.
'I expect to pass through this life but once. If, therefore, there can be any kindnesses I can show, or any good thing I can do to any fellow beings, let me do it now. Let me not defer or neglect it, for I shall not pass this way again.'
—A.B. Hegeman"

Thank you, Julie! You are an extraordinary friend!

Resources:

Love Your Life To Death by Yvonne Heath.

https://www.psychologytoday.com/us/blog/the-art-and-science-aging-well/202006/shifting-our-perspective-death

https://www.medicalnewstoday.com/articles/308447#:~:-text=Discussing%20death&text=According%20to%20an%20Institute%20of,%2C%20cultural%20and%20ethical%20standards."

Our Changing Views: Is Death a Grim or Gentle Reaper?

*I do not fear death. I had been dead for billions
and billions of years before I was born and had not
suffered the slightest inconvenience from it.*
—Mark Twain.

According to the Cleveland Clinic, "During death, your body's vital functions stop entirely. Your heart no longer beats, your breath stops, and your brain stops functioning. Studies suggest that brain activity may continue several minutes after a person has been declared dead. Still, brain activity isn't the same as consciousness or awareness."[26]

The Chapman University Survey of American Fears Wave 7 (2020/2021) lists the fear of losing a loved one as the number two fear among Americans. The number one fear was corrupt government officials. Really! Look it up! Hmm, what does that say about us?

In Chapman's 2022 survey, corrupt government officials was still first on the list, but loved ones becoming seriously ill came in second place, Russia using nuclear weapons was in third place which pushed the fear of losing a loved one to death down into fourth place.

---

[26] my.clevelandclinic.org.

Another survey from SafeHome.org lists loved ones dying, loved ones becoming seriously ill, and becoming terminally ill as the number one, two, and seven most common fears.

I think it would be safe to say that death typically makes the top ten of most surveys where fear is concerned.

Fear is described by *Psychology Today* as a response to physical and emotional danger and is vital to protect ourselves from legitimate threats. It was particularly important in ancient times when towns and villages were routinely raided, and life was frequently cut short due to violence rather than disease. However, when many of us can expect to live until our body parts wear out or a bacterial or viral invader attacks us, fear can still be useful in terms of prevention but may complicate our prognosis. Chronic fear can weaken our immune system, cause cardiovascular damage, gastrointestinal damage, and even lead to accelerated aging and premature death, according to the University of Minnesota.[27]

So, what can we do to minimize the fear of death and dying? According to the book, *Overcoming the Fear of Death: Through Each of the Four Main Belief Systems* by Kelvin H. Chin, the four main belief systems about death are:

1. No belief in an afterlife
2. Afraid of heaven or hell
3. Looking forward to heaven
4. Belief in past lives

The book also discusses hybrids of those four beliefs. No matter what your belief is, making the best legacy possible while you are here and preparing your loved ones for life after you are gone is still a good idea.

Maybe we should all consider death simply a graduation from life.

---

[27] https://www.takingcharge.csh.umn.edu/impact-fear-and-anxiety.

According to PEW Research Center, 17 percent of Americans do not believe in an afterlife, while 73 percent believe in heaven. Those numbers would imply that the remaining 10 percent have either a hybrid view of the afterlife or believe in reincarnation; the study did not specify numbers but expressed some of these views as short answers. The study also found that almost three-quarters of all US adults (72 percent) think it is possible for people to have "a near-death experience" in which their spirit actually leaves their body.[28]

One of the first things I learned in my death doula studies was the importance of being knowledgeable and sensitive to the beliefs of others. I can't help someone navigate through the dying process if I don't understand what they believe will happen to them when their heart stops beating, and their brain waves stop.

Yvonne Heath wrote a wonderful book, *Love Your Life to Death* which is a must-read for everyone. In her book, she discusses her encounters with dying patients in different cultures, especially their views on death. In one instance, she shares the views of a Buddhist patient, "In Buddhist philosophy, life is eternal; it has no beginning and no end. We experience one lifetime after another... Consequently, death is nothing to fear."

As you may have guessed, when it comes to my belief system, I am clearly in the "looking forward-to-heaven" camp but have great respect for those with other views.

As a Christian, I believe that I will be reunited with my mother, my son, and my husband at my death. After Eric died, I read the book *Heaven* by Randy Alcorn. It helped me to cope with the loss of my son by envisioning him in a loving and beautiful place. Please remember that for many years organized religions questioned the ability of someone who had taken his or her own life to ever attain a happy afterlife.

---

[28] https://www.pewresearch.org/religion/2021/11/23/views-on-the-afterlife/.

This was the case when my mother died in 1974. No church was willing to hold a service for this amazingly loving, kind, and godly woman. I remember standing next to her casket in a funeral home that was dripping in shame and woe. It was a humiliating end for a woman who loved so much. There was no sacred music. All tones were hushed. At seventeen, the physical loss of my mother, who suffered from mental illness throughout her life, was compounded by the fear that she was still suffering in the afterlife.

The years between 1974 and 2009 saw an extraordinary change in the church's views on mental illness. Although taking any life is still considered a grave matter, by 2009, most Christian churches gave the benefit of the doubt that someone who had taken their own life, especially if they were suffering from depression or other mental illness, may not have understood the full repercussions of his or her actions. There was also a significantly increased focus on God's grace for all of us sinners.

Eric's funeral was very different than my mother's funeral home viewing (see Legacy of Encouragement Chapter). It was an amazing show of love and respect. Although Eric was a college student at the time of his death, his former all boys Catholic high school, including students, teachers, administrators, and the entire orchestra, showed up in force on a school day. I was still in shock, and there are parts that I don't remember, but one image that I will never forget and one of the most amazing gifts a grieving mother could receive was the aisles of our church packed with young men, most with tears in their eyes, standing at attention and saluting the coffin of my son as it passed by. Eric made an impact in his short nineteen years that most people fail to make in a much longer lifetime. I can never thank those boys enough for the honor they paid to my son and the comfort they gave to my family.

The Baptists showed up in force too. Eric was part of the worship team, and the team leader, who had terminal cancer, spoke in Eric's honor. Our pastor, Roger Thompson, very clearly and pointedly discussed the topic of mental illness and suicide and the impact it left behind, but most importantly, on God's mercy. Our large church sanctuary was full, and the gym and a number of overflow rooms were also filled to capacity with video access to the sanctuary. Even after thirteen years, I still meet people who attended Eric's funeral and didn't even know us at the time. A few weeks after the service, I got a letter from the Archbishop expressing gratitude for the impact Eric's funeral had on the students in attendance (see "Legacy of Encouragement Chapter").

About a month after Eric's death, I visited St. Thomas Academy for just a brief moment. At that exact time, I just "happened" to run into one of the priests who served the school and who knew Eric. He was retired at this time, terminally ill himself, and in need of portable oxygen. He rushed over to me, grabbed my hand, and with tears in his eyes, expressed his sorrow over the death of the "dancing bear" (his name for Eric). He told me that he was sure that he would see him soon in heaven and would give him a big hug from his family. I can't tell you the comfort that encounter gave me, and I don't believe it was a coincidence that I met him in the hallway.

Since I believe that our relationship with God is a personal one, the differences in theology between the Catholic and Protestant churches is not important to me, but the kindness and support that I received after Eric's death from both churches was remarkable and helped in my emotional recovery from not only Eric's death but my mother's as well.

I have to also mention the support of the community at Columbia University. Eric had been a wonderful student and very active on campus as a member of the student government and the jazz program. He was most known for his enthusiastic greetings and hugs and playing piano all around campus. The university held a candlelit ceremony for him and eventually placed a memorial shadbush and plaque in honor of Eric in front of the engineering building, making him an honorary member of the class of 2012. We will be forever grateful for the support given to us by the students and faculty at Columbia.

Community support after the death of a loved one is critical. When my husband Jim died, both times (see chapter one), we were still in the throes of COVID lockdowns. Churches were just beginning to hold funerals again, and Jim's was the third to be held since the lockdowns at our church. Pastor Brent did a wonderful job officiating. The number of people allowed was limited, and we were all spaced out for safety, however, since it was taped, over eight hundred people were able to see his service. The burial at Fort Snelling was also delayed and included immediate family only.

But at least I had that; I can't imagine the suffering incurred by families during the height of the lockdown when there was no opportunity for a funeral and no one to mourn with. We need other people to comfort us when we are suffering.

So, are we afraid of dying? A 2019 study by Statista revealed that 25 percent of Americans are not at all afraid of dying, 7 percent don't know if they are afraid, and the remaining 69 percent report at least some fear.[29]

Before Eric died, I would have classified myself in the "somewhat fearful of death" category, but at this point in my life, I am definitely in the "not at all afraid" category. Where are you? If you are afraid, why are you afraid?

Let's take a nonjudgmental look at the statistics as we know them, at least about our earthly views of death.

About 17 percent of Americans believe that there is no

---

[29] https://www.statista.com/statistics/959347/fear-of-death-in-the-us/

afterlife. They believe that when our heart stops and our brainwaves cease, so do we. A 2009 Pew Research poll found that 41 percent of scientists do not believe in a higher power. Since the Pew number for those in the general population who do not believe in a higher power matches the 17 percent of Americans who do not believe in an afterlife, this led me to assume that most people who do not believe in a higher power also do not believe in an afterlife.[30] In the PEW study, 51 percent of scientists believed in a higher power, and 7 percent didn't know or refused to answer.

One interesting study by the University of Chicago showed that 76 percent of physicians believed in God, and 59 percent believed in some sort of an afterlife. So it looks like you can't make the assumption that someone who believes in a higher power automatically believes in an afterlife. I find this fascinating! I also find it interesting that the University of Chicago researchers were surprised at how many physicians believed in God. This number was higher than expected, according to the study.[31]

Whether you believe in God or not, most people characterize death as a "Grim Reaper." I think we need to reconsider that. If death is related to violence, then I can understand the association, but I believe that the actual moment of death itself is not violent or grim; I believe it to be peaceful. I think death is a Gentle Reaper.

Resources:
I've Seen the End of You: A Neurosurgeon's Look at Faith, Doubt, and the Things We Think We Know, by W. Lee Warren, MD

---

[30] https://www.pewresearch.org/religion/2009/11/05/scientists-and-belief/.

[31] https://www.uchicagomedicine.org/forefront/news/survey-shows-that-physicians-are-more-religious-than-expected.

https://www.chapman.edu/wilkinson/research-centers/bab-
    bie-center/_files/Babbie%20center%20fear2021/blogpost-
    americas-top-fears-2020_-21-final.pdf
https://blogs.chapman.edu/wilkinson/category/fear-index/
https://blogs.chapman.edu/wilkinson/2022/10/14/
    the-top-10-fears-in-america-2022/
https://www.safehome.org/home-safety/american-fear-study/

Life After Death?

*People into hard sciences, neurophysiology, often ignore
a core philosophical question: 'What is the relationship
between our unique, inner experience of conscious awareness
and material substance?' The answer is we don't know,
and some people are so terrified to say 'I don't know.'*
—*Raymond Moody M.D.*

One of my new pastimes is watching YouTube videos in which
learned scientists discuss the phenomenon of near-death experiences (NDEs). The University of Virginia has done extensive
research on the topic, and they even have a research branch
in the Department of Psychiatry and Neurobehavioral Sciences,
called the Division of Perceptual Studies, which has investigated
the question "is there life after death?" for over 50 years.[32]

Studies show that around 15 percent of people who have suffered cardiac arrest have been resuscitated. Pim Van Lommel
MD studied 344 patients in the Netherlands who had suffered
cardiac arrest, and 62 or 18 percent had some sort of NDE.[33]

In *Afterlife*,[34] physician and author Raymond Moody, who
wrote the groundbreaking book *Life after Life,* was interviewed.

---

[32] https://www.youtube.com/watch?v=0AtTM9hgCDw.

[33] https://www.thelancet.com/journals/lancet/article/PIIS0140673601071008/fulltext.

[34] https://youtu.be/8aWveRxcVP8.

He described death as entering a whole new area of existence or conscience that is so different that our language cannot even describe it. He also said that the most important thing we can do when we are alive is to learn how to love. He believes that, when he dies, he will be seeing events in his life again, but in the eyes of the people he has interacted with. Wow! Maybe we should start thinking about that perspective now! I believe Raymond Moody. Hmmm, could we make a heaven here on Earth by just loving people?

Another YouTube video that is intriguing is a debate between a skeptical neurointensivist, and an emergency medicine expert who would like to change the term describing this phenomenon from NDE (Near Death Experience) to ADE (Actual Death Experience).[35] It shows rational, educated people with different interpretations of how and when death occurs. My favorite part is the respect these esteemed specialists show to a view that is different from their own. That mutual respect is something that we all need to adopt. Frequently I find that when it comes to emotional topics like death, those on one side of the debate have a tendency to disparage or write off those on the other side of the debate as uneducated or gullible or not willing to face the facts. I believe that asking people, "What do you think happens to you after you die?" and listening intently with the goal of understanding can open up dialogues that can be enriching to both parties.

It is interesting to see how many people have experienced either a near-death experience or a deathbed vision or experience.

According to the article, "Deathbed Visions: Part I" by Marilyn A. Mendoza, PhD, "A deathbed vision (DBV) is a vision or experience that the individual has before dying. It may occur

---

[35] https://www.youtube.com/watch?v=qviKvjNecCQ.

immediately before death or days or even weeks prior. Patients have reported visions of dead family members, religious figures, and/or beautiful scenery." The author reported that 57 percent of the visions reported to her were of deceased relatives, most frequently the mother. She goes on to say "Whether you believe these events are hallucinations from a dying brain or are true spiritual experiences, the impact on the dying, the medical staff, and family can be profound and help soften the grieving process.[36]

Jackie Pederson, RN, who has worked with the dying for over thirty years, tells the story of one of her patients sitting up in her bed, her face beaming, who asked, "Jesus! There he is, can you see Him?" Jackie also remembers a dear friend who died in her arms and told her that she would let Jackie know that she "made it" by coming back as "the weirdest bird you have ever seen." Sure enough, when Jackie got home and sat down to dinner, she spotted the weirdest bird she had ever seen at her bird feeder.

One of the most famous examples of a deathbed experience (or vision) was Steve Jobs, whose last words were, "Oh wow! Oh wow! Oh wow!" I would love to know what he was responding to!

Many healthcare professionals who I have talked to relate this fairly common occurrence of patients "seeing" loved ones who are dead, encouraging them during their last days, and sometimes even giving them an accurate timeline as to when they will go "home." Don't take my word for this; ask the next hospice worker you meet or research this on your own. I have been meeting with a widows group weekly since Jim's death, and six of the nine widows report supernatural experiences occurring around death. Before I started asking people, I had no idea this was so common. Of course, nine widows do not make a big

---

[36] https://www.psychologytoday.com/us/blog/understanding-grief/201610/deathbed-visions-part-i.

enough group to conduct any type of statistically significant study! The next time you are with your friends, try asking them what they think will happen when they die! You will find the answers varied and *fascinating*!

Why do I believe there is a God and therefore a life after death? Our beliefs are a response to our life experiences. Here are some of mine:

My mom gave me my faith when I was four years old. She taught me to believe in a loving God and to turn to Him in times both good and bad. Talking about God was an everyday occurrence. I tried to live by the two most important commandments, "Love God" and "Love People." This may seem simplistic, but it gave me strength and courage that I know I would not have without my faith.

I have not had any miraculous experiences myself, but I have had a few what I call "almost miracles" when I felt a supernatural strength help me.

The first time I felt this inner strength was when I was about eighteen years old and in college. I was on my own, struggling to pay my way through college with three jobs. I was also clinically depressed and had just lost my mother to suicide. I was approached by an organization I will just call "The Cult" in a parking lot at a mall with the promise to get me back into a psychologically healthy mind with a program that was very reasonably priced. Anyone who has suffered from an emotional illness knows that you will do almost anything to remove that pain from your brain. I started attending weekly seminars, but then they said I needed further appointments, and this time, it would cost more. I continued for a while and then ran out of money. Then, "The Cult" asked me to join them. They would offer me a protective "family" of cult members, and I could work for them full-time. I could then continue my mental processing where, eventually, I would be freed from all of my sufferings.

At this point, I started to get a bit suspicious about their interest in me. Also, I did not have the money they wanted. (They suggested that I use my college tuition money.) When I failed to join with the soft approach, they brought me into a room with a man dressed in a black suit who spent over two hours interrogating me. He told me that if I didn't continue with the program, I would die like my mother from suicide in an insane asylum (his exact words.) At this time in my life, I was gullible. I was respectful of authority. I followed directions. I believed what authority figures told me.

However, somehow, on this day, I responded with a completely rational reply to every argument he used in his attempt to bring me into the sect. I had no idea where these answers came from. Every so often, the man would become exasperated and leave for a moment to an adjacent room. He would come back with another angle and a new reason I needed to leave college and follow this group. Finally, he had had enough. As he gruffly escorted me out the door, I got a glimpse into the room to which he would retreat. In that room were two men, also in black suits, who were sitting behind a monitor with a clear view of the empty chair I had just been sitting in. Three men were working together to trap me into joining "The Cult." I was a lonely, gullible, people-pleasing eighteen-year-old, with no family to care about me, who had just out argued three adult males. I know that I did not accomplish that alone; it was the first time I felt the presence of something beyond what I could see.

A few years later, in dental school, Jim and I were white water rafting. At one point, I fell out of the raft and got caught in a river hydraulic (water spinning around under a big rock), and for a moment, I thought I was going to die. My life started flashing before my eyes in a very calm and very strange way, but fortunately, I was soon spat out by the water. I didn't think much of the event except as something rather unusual until I started reading about near-death experiences others reported. My adventure under the water would definitely not classify as a near-death experience, as I was not unconscious (just getting there), but my faith in a higher power and belief in an afterlife were strengthened.

In the spring of 1996, my sister-in-law, Mary, called me as I was waiting for a call from my fourteen-year-old daughter, Hillary. Hillary's boyfriend had just broken up with her at a Christian youth camp, and she was devastated. I told her to try to stick it out, but that she could call me at any time, and I would drive down to pick her up. She was distraught when I talked to her, and I was worried. When I explained this to Mary, she prayed with me and asked God to tell Hillary how much He loved her. It was a great prayer, but I was still worried about my daughter. When I picked her up at the assigned time the next day, she was smiling and happy, and I was relieved that she seemed to have gotten through this heartache. When she got into the car, she told me that she had had a strange experience. Just at about the time Mary had been praying, her group was in devotions. The leader had asked the group to picture themselves at the foot of the cross of Jesus and wonder what He would have said to them. "Mom," Hillary announced, "It was strange... I felt that Jesus came right down from that cross and told me how much He loved me." I still get goosebumps when I think of that story. Mary also reported having a near-death experience as she was lying unconscious after an automobile accident. Mary said that she was not ready to die and asked to come back. Mary had some interesting spiritual connections.

When my son Eric was eight years old, Jim was driving him back from a karate lesson, and Eric was asleep and reclined in the front seat of the car. Suddenly their car was hit head-on by a young seventeen-year-old man, who had just gotten his license, with a friend in the front seat.

Eric remembered waking up after the crash to see his dad slumped over the steering wheel. Eric reported that there was an angel sitting in between them. But this didn't, he reported, look like a "regular angel." He was a bit stout and had long blonde hair. This angel didn't talk to Eric in the regular way, through words, but he communicated through his mind and said to him, "Don't be afraid, your dad is not dead: he is asleep, and you need to wake him up and get out of the car." Jim did not remember the accident, but does remember Eric waking him up and telling him that he had to get out of the car. When Jim got out of the car, he went to the other car and pulled the boys out, but they were both dead. Eric was taken away by bystanders and eventually to an ambulance. When Eric was asked when he saw the angel for the last time, Eric said that as he was being ministered to by the good Samaritans and eventually paramedics and police officers, he saw the angel standing next to his dad with his arm around him and another bystander as Jim was crying over the boys' bodies. Later, when I read Billie Graham's book about angels, I was amazed to find out that Rev. Graham described angels as looking like regular people and communicating with us telepathically, not necessarily with words. I was not only comforted by Eric's report of angels as an eight-year-old little boy, but was doubly comforted by Billy Graham's book years after Eric had died.

Jim and my daughters had vivid dreams about Eric after he died. Jim had several, each one with a different message. I only had one unusual experience in which the phone rang, and I picked it up and heard Eric on the other end saying in an enthusiastic voice, "Hi, Mom!" I woke up in a start as it felt so real. Every mom can tell how her child is with just a word, and Eric's greeting said, "I am doing great." Other people had vivid dreams about Eric as well. When Jim was having his first heart surgery, I was waiting with sisters-in-laws Judy and Sue and daughters Ashley and Hillary. Our niece, Jordan, was a nurse at Mayo and joined us just after her shift was finished. The surgery was supposed to last four hours, and we were on hour nine. The tension was high. Jordan then said, "I didn't know if I should tell you or not about a dream I had after Eric died, but this seems like a good time." She then went on to say that Eric came to her in a dream shortly after his death and asked her to tell us that his death was not our fault in any way, it was an accident, he was sorry, and he was in a good place. I felt like a bolt of lightning had just hit me. Not only was that dream comforting because of the message, but I had been told of the exact same dream from one of Eric's friends from Columbia while she was in New York, as well as a high school friend who had a similar vision while in church on Ash Wednesday in New Orleans. He was attending Loyola University. Three reports of "Eric Visions" from three unrelated people in three different parts of the country did not seem like a coincidence to me.

When my daughter Hillary told us she was having twins, we were elated! Two grandchildren all at once. But once Jim found out that Hillary was now considered a high-risk pregnancy, he began to get fearful. He worried constantly about the babies until one night, he had a dream that the two girls were going to be just fine. He had a vision of two little girls with long white/blonde hair, about four years old, in matching red dresses swinging in a swing and laughing and chasing each other around. That dream changed his outlook and took his worry away completely. Jim looked forward to their birth just like the rest of us. When the girls were born, Jim was a little confused. Their hair was not white; it was brown. He said, "Wow, I was sure that dream was real, but they look different." About three years later, I was getting ready to wrap my Christmas gifts for the girls. I found both girls beautiful long dresses with hot-pink flowers. Jim walked by and said, "Oh my goodness, those are the dresses I saw in my dream!" "Jim," I said, "these dresses aren't red; they are hot pink!" "Kim," Jim said, "That color is a lot closer to red than it is to pink," and he was right. By this time, the twins' hair had turned from brown to white. Their Christmas present dresses turned out to be their favorites, and at their fourth birthday party, they chose these dresses to wear. Sure enough, that day, we saw two little white-haired girls in their "reddish" dresses chasing each other, giggling, and swinging on the swings. Jim smiled all day long.

A few years later, my dear friend, Carol, was dying. Jim woke up in the middle of the night and said, "Carol's dead." At about the same time, the phone rang, and it was Carol's husband giving me the news. Jim said that he felt Carol's spirit rush by him. I have to admit that I was a little hurt that Carol didn't rush by me, but (if I am right about the afterlife) I will discuss that with her later.

I described my most recent supernatural experience (when Jim died the first time on Eric's thirty-first birthday) in the "Your Life Is Your Legacy" chapter. You may think that not having a heartbeat or taking a breath for twenty minutes, still being able to think clearly, and then dying peacefully on the day after Eric's birthday was simply an unusual medical phenomenon and coincidence, but I am respectfully sticking with my belief of divine intervention on that one.

While I have personally not experienced a near-death experience or had a supernatural vision, I believe credible people with no ulterior motive who describe them. My response, whether they conform to my understanding of the divine or not, is: FASCINATING! Some of us believe in a higher power, visions, and an afterlife, and some of us don't. That is okay. When it comes to death, we need to be understanding that people are different in their beliefs. We will find out soon enough! No matter what we believe about what happens after we die, we can all agree that we will, in fact, die. Whether you believe in an afterlife or not, the scientifically accepted understanding that NDEs exist should at least help us understand the death process and that, from the vast majority of reports, it is not something to be afraid of. Why not get prepared for whatever comes next? Alexander Graham Bell once said, "Before anything, preparation is the key to success." To help you prepare to make your parting less painful for those you leave behind, Part Three is a workbook that includes a checklist. Let's get started; your survivors will thank you!

Resources:

Consciousness Beyond Life, The Science of the Near-Death Experience by Pim Van Lommel MD.

Every Moment Holy by Douglas McKelvey

Every Moment Holy Volume II, Death Grief and Hope, by Douglas McKelvey

Love Your Life to Death by Yvonne Heath.

Life After Life by Raymond Moody Jr. MD.

Overcoming the Fear of Death: Through Each of the Four Main Belief Systems by Kelvin H. Chin.

https://www.youtube.com/watch?v=rbnBe-vXGQM (*I See Dead People*, Dr. Christopher Kerr).

https://www.youtube.com/watch?v=4RGizqsLumo (*Life After Death*, UVA Panel).

https://www.youtube.com/watch?v=fVoOScxhJ9M (*Surviving Death*).

https://www.youtube.com/watch?v=zPCvuva2deU (*Experiencing Death*).

https://www.youtube.com/watch?v=vg8WAv0YT9c (*More to Dying Than Meets the Eye*).

https://youtu.be/8aWveRxcVP8 (*Afterlife*, Paul Perry, Jeff Long).

Part Three:
The Death Prepper's Workbook

The Time to Start Prepping is Now

*If you believe you can accomplish everything by 'cramming'
at the eleventh hour, by all means, don't lift a finger
now. But you may think twice about beginning to
build your ark once it has already started raining.*
—Max Brooks

Understanding your relationship with death is important, but so are the steps to organize your estate and your final wishes. I firmly believe that one of the best gifts you can leave to your family is the ability to maintain good relationships after your death. Having all your affairs in order is one way to show your love for them.

In 1980, my husband was thirty-one years old and in the National Guard. His commanding officer ordered the men in his unit to get their affairs in order because they were likely to be involved in a dangerous overseas mission. The world was in turmoil then and apparently on the brink of war. Fortunately, the war and the hazardous mission never materialized. We had very few affairs to get in order as we were poor students. Financially we had nothing, but I would have much appreciated some emotional preparedness had Jim been deployed.

When Jim died at age seventy, I was sad to see how his death negatively affected not only me but our entire family, especially our precious grandchildren. This project focuses on financially preparing our survivors and emotionally preparing them for a time when we are not physically present in their lives. Many of us do some preparation, such as writing a will, but end up working on the hard stuff only after a devastating diagnosis gives us an imminent deadline! Wouldn't it be wonderful to live our lives to the fullest without the burden of knowing that there are things we need to do for our survivors that we have not yet done?

The plan is to develop a program in which we concentrate on building our legacy of love for those we will leave behind. Using our existing social groups (book clubs, church groups, or other groups) to provide moral support and loving accountability, I hope we can encourage each other to complete these essential tasks. No judgment, just help!!!

This workbook includes the **Death Prepper's Goal Setting Guide,** which divides the tasks needed to assist your loved ones in negotiating their way through your immediate pre-death and post-death issues. Do you have a healthcare directive to help your loved ones understand your end-of-life healthcare wishes? Healthcare directives allow you to die how you wish, even when you cannot express yourself. I am so glad that my husband had his in place. It helped me ensure that Jim died the way he wanted, and that knowledge gave me peace. Having your wishes expressed in writing helps prevent guilt and deep-seated family disagreements.

After you are gone, will your family have to haggle their way through your possessions? Not if you have a will with clear directions on dividing your personal effects. By developing a legacy folder or binder with your passwords, financial information, insurance accounts, funeral, and legacy information, you will show your love for your survivors by helping them navigate through the weeks and months after you die. Additional information is provided in the area of Last Will and Testaments, Healthcare Directives, writing an Obituary, and planning your funeral.

The **Death Prepper's Emotional Help for Survivors Checklist** is designed to help emotionally prepare your loved ones for a time when you are no longer physically present in their lives. Following the checklist is detailed information about the five tasks of mourning, how to make videos, books, or letters about your family history, as well as how to write reconciliation, apology, or love letters to your survivors. Although our society focuses on possessions and money as our legacy, our most important legacy is the love we leave behind. This part of the workbook focuses on ensuring that your love for your family is permanently documented.

Some of us are uncomfortable talking with others about these issues, and if you are one of these people, fear not! The directions for completing these tasks are written for individual consumption; the groups just help with accountability.

Death Prepper's Goal-Setting Guide

Directions: Cross off tasks you do not want to do. Check off tasks already accomplished. Work with your group (or individually) to develop a plan to finish all the tasks you wish to do. Three asterisks will follow subjects where detailed information is provided later on.

Death Prepper's Checklist
___ have a discussion with your family regarding your wishes
___ name of executor
___ name of accountant
___ name of attorney
___ name of tax preparer
___ name of a financial advisor
___ name of health care provider
___ prepare a power of attorney
___ Living Will/Health Care Directive***
___ Last Will and Testament***
___ personal information (Legal name, maiden name, social security number, birthplace, spouse's name, former spouse's name, children's names)
___ location of will, passport, driver's license, birth certificate, keys, marriage certificate (Ideally, have copies of all important documents in your legacy folder/binder)
___ location of valuables

___ safe and combination or location of keys

___ historical information (parents' names and birthplaces)

___ insurance for burial expenses, if applicable

___ employee benefits

___ make sure appropriate beneficiaries are listed for bank accounts, retirement accounts, life insurance, etc., to ensure access to your funds

___ organ/tissue donation***

___ list of investments

___ real estate owned or leased and details

___ cars (VIN number, title/ lease location, key location, make, year, and model)

___ boats and other vehicles and identifying information, location of keys

___ firearms (location and description)

___ list of passwords

___ list of bank accounts

___ list of credit cards numbers, account numbers, online usernames, and passwords

___ list of email and social media usernames and passwords

___ list of life insurance policies

___ list utilities (gas, electric, water, phone)

___ health insurance information (keep a copy of your card in your folder)

___ access to documents plan

___ share legacy information***

___ decide upon living wake, funeral, both?***

___ religious affiliation, home church

___ choose and arrange burial***

    ___ traditional

    ___ cremation

    ___ natural

___ burial at sea

___ aquamation

___ composting

___ sky burial

___ become a diamond, cryonics, etc.

___ space burial

___ secure burial plot, share any pre-arrangement activities

___ military service, if applicable

___ if a veteran, secure the appropriate papers for burial benefits

___ select pallbearers

___ write an obituary (or give information to someone else to write)***

___ select your obituary picture***

___ if a business owner, ensure your business is ready for the transition

___ if a business owner, business name, location, bank, accountant, attorney, contracts, employees names and contact information, lease, keys, user names and passwords, business credit cards, financial records, accounts receivables, income stream

___ if a business owner/partner, make sure your heirs understand transition plans

___ list of people to notify and social media announcement (Perhaps develop a calling system)

___ make your own meme-orial (A meme is basically a short video or image or piece of writing that is usually humorous and spreads rapidly on the Internet. To learn more about memes', check out https://www.lifewire.com/what-is-a-meme-2483702)

___ list of creditors: itemize personal loans, names, detailed information

___ notify parties included in your will

___ give directions or fill out the forms necessary for securing the property you own such as

   ___ stopping the mail

   ___ putting you on the deceased, do not contact list

   ___ cancel services etc., driver's license, SSN, passport

   ___ important bills that need to be paid

   ___ closing digital accounts

___ compile a list of assets

___ list the location of important items

___ address the payment of income and real estate taxes

___ develop a system to distribute assets not covered by your will

___ pet names, license info, veterinarian

___ list pet names, license information, veterinarian

___ work out pet care for when you are gone. Give special instructions

___ set aside payment for someone to "clean up" what remains (Refer to "The Legacy of Shedding" chapter)

___ specify location and information about storage units

___ if you have a monument, decide what you want to put on it***

___ Other_____

___ Other_____

___ Other_____

Resources:
The Legacy Planning and Conversation Guide by Chris Bentley
https://www.amazon.com/Legacy-Planning-Conversation-Guide
-Life/dp/B08732LCCK/ref=sr_1_3?crid=13VDM5GE9Y-
RVG&keywords=Chris+Bentley&qid=1685242346&sprefix-
=chris+bentley%2Caps%2C116&sr=8-3

Love Your Life to Death: How to Plan and Prepare for the End of Life So You Can Live Fully Now by Yvonne Heath.

EndInMindProject.org

WingsforWidows.org

https://time.com/5640494/why-you-need-to-make-a-when-i-die-file-before-its-too-late/.

https://www.investopedia.com/articles/retirement/10/estate-planning-checklist.asp.

Before All Is Said and Done: Practical Advice on Living and Dying Well, Pat Miles, Made for Success Publishing, Issaquah, WA 2022.

I'm Dead. Now What?; Important Information about My Belongings, Business Affairs, and Wishes, Peter Pauper Press, Inc., White Plains N.Y. 2015.

Please Don't Die! But if You Do, What Do I Do Next? Kurt J. Grube and Keith S. Grube Esq., Kurt Grube, Wykoff, NJ 2012.

When I'm Gone: Death Planner Organizer, The Guides Press 2021.

Because I Love You: Christian Legacy Organizer, Dr. Brian Kluth.

Having a Family Discussion

Talking about our death is hard. But not talking about what is inevitable while we are still here (and our brains are still functioning) may result in unnecessary pain, suffering, conflict, and chaos for those who live on. Let's face it; we do not like to talk about life and death decisions, and certainly not when it is *our* life and death we are talking about. Be prepared for different reactions from different family members.

Your family needs to know where your death-prepping information is; they need to know the philosophy behind your decisions, and they need to know how and where you want to spend your last days. One advantage of this discussion is that you will learn how your family responds to your wishes. If you spend the time and effort to have a comprehensive death planning folder in place, what good will it do if no one knows where to access it? Also, what if your loved ones object to how you wish to spend your last days? Having this discussion will allow you to reinforce your wishes and/or make any changes you feel are necessary. The debate over seeking every measure possible to sustain life or taking the hospice route may become emotional, but better to have it while you can participate (as the ultimate decision maker) rather than when you are no longer able to make or express such decisions.

One of the best books I have read on the subject of aging was the bestselling book, *Being Mortal: Medicine and What Matters in the End* by Atul Gawande, MD. It might be a good idea to give this book as a gift at Thanksgiving and engage in a family discussion around Christmas. Or you can use other traditional family gathering time or schedule a meeting specifically to discuss these issues. You could even suggest the meeting as a wonderful Mother's or Father's day gift to you. There are also numerous YouTube videos, streaming movies, or this book to help educate your family. The American Psychological Association has a great podcast you can share; https://www.apa.org/news/podcasts/speaking-of-psychology/talking-death.

Don't be disappointed if you meet resistance when discussing the future. All you can do is try. If someone is completely dismissive, then consider expressing your views in a letter. The important thing is to do your best!

Until now, we have been discussing your death, but what if you fear your parent or grandparent has not planned well or has not talked to you about their desires, and you would like them to express their wishes to you? Why not ask them?

This process can be relatively simple if they are open to discussion or extremely difficult if they are not. As we age, the thought of losing our independence or, worse yet, dying can be terrifying. We know in our minds that our death will happen someday, but we may not accept that it will happen to us anytime soon. Broaching the topic of your loved one's death may cause an emotional reaction that you are both unprepared for. Find a quiet time with just the two of you. Be gentle; this is a tough issue for many.

One discussion will not be enough. Be the engine that starts the conversation and strive to keep the discussions open, respectful, and informative. Only you can do this. Don't procrastinate. We think we will always have time, but at some point, for all of us, our time will run out. Will your family be meeting for a big event soon? Is there an appropriate time you can schedule a "planning for the future" meeting? By framing this as a "future planning" meeting rather than a "death planning" meeting, you may reduce the discomfort! Don't wait! You can do this!!

Resources:
One of the best resources is *Your Conversation Starter Guide* available from the Institute for Healthcare Development. I recommend that everyone at least check this out! It is excellent:

https://theconversationproject.org.
Being Mortal: Medicine and What Matters in the End by Atul Gawande, MD.
https://www.artofdyingwell.org/talking-about-death/.
https://theconversation.com/us/topics/talking-about-death-and-dying-1905.
https://youtu.be/RtFFT4zjyTM.

Your Last Will and Testament: Where Do Your Valuables Go?

I am a dentist, not an attorney; the information in this chapter is not legal advice, just observation. Please see an appropriately licensed attorney to write your Last Will and Testament and advise you on estate planning.

We are all aware of families torn apart because parents or grand-parents never quite got around to writing a Last Will and Testament. There are also many families who were so surprised at the division of property that they contested the will. In some cases, the cost of adjudicating such situations left the families penniless and the lawyers rich. If we love those we leave behind, shouldn't we ease the transition by providing a solid framework to divide our possessions?

Jim and I wanted to ensure that our deaths did not damage our daughters' beautiful relationship. We wrote our wills with a fifty-fifty split and sent them to both girls to examine before we signed them. Our mandate was: "Speak now or forever hold your peace."

After my will was signed, I sat down with my daughters, brought any jewelry I had to the table, and let each girl choose a piece in turn. The choices were written down and attached to my will so there would be no controversy after my death. I thought there would be many other possessions my girls would want and consider valuable, but the sad reality is they do not want my stuff. Like many baby boomers, I thought at least the beautiful china sets I had collected over forty-four years of marriage would be considered precious heirlooms. They are not. I have heard rumors that beautiful china is becoming appreciated again. I hope that rumor is true.

When your survivors are already established and have their own homes, it is common for them to look at the disposal of your property as a major burden ("The Legacy of Shedding").

The fact is that I raised two beautiful daughters with their own homes and their own tastes and no room for additional furniture or accessories. I can choose to celebrate their independence or bemoan the fate of my "stuff." I choose to celebrate my independent daughters.

I am leaving some "clean-up" money in my will specifically designated to cover disposal after my family has selected the valuables they want. This could then be used to pay a family member or professional company to hold an estate sale and take the pressure off my children.

Compared to many, my family was easy. My children are self-sufficient, and there are only two. They also get along well. If a family has a special needs child that may require an income, if the family is blended, or if one member of the family has worked to promote a family business, it may get complicated. There are many other complicating factors, such as kids who don't get along, no apparent heirs, or the deceased wishes to donate a large sum to charity. You can do a lot to ease problems following your death by helping your heirs understand the thinking behind your decisions before your death through letter of intent. (See below, next chapter.) You don't need to share specific amounts unless you wish to, but surprises, such as uneven distribution among siblings, a large charitable donation, or unexpected inheritors, are easier to accept if they are logical in nature and explained before your death.

It is also important to consider what happens if there is a divorce and a remarriage or remarriage after one spouse dies. My husband Jim was an extrovert extraordinaire. He did not like being alone. We all knew that if I died first, Jim would want to remarry. I just asked him not to look for my replacement until after my funeral. We considered this possibility when we wrote our wills. The most important possession that had sentimental value for us was our lake home. We built it to be a retirement home, but due to illness, disability, and our need to be near our grandchildren, our condo took over that role. I may move to the lake at some point, but we now use it as a short-term rental to cover the costs of maintenance. The girls wanted to make sure our cabin stayed with the family, and we agreed. In our will, the cabin is in a trust in my name. If I died first, Jim could live in the cabin until his death, but the ownership would belong to our daughters. In this way, the cabin would be protected from being lost to the family that built it. These are important things to consider, as well as a prenuptial or postnuptial agreement when getting remarried so that there are no surprises for the new spouse or the children.

Your attorney will draw up your will to include many things, such as your family history: are you married, are there children, how you will pay your debts, who will receive your assets and how they will receive them, guardianship of your children, and who you want as the executor to manage the distribution of the assets.

Having an easily authenticated will drafted by a knowledgeable attorney will help you avoid much of the cost of probate. The American Bar Association has some great tips.[37]

Probate is the court-supervised process that your will undergoes after you pass away. If you have a will, this process is much

---

[37] https://www.americanbar.org/groups/real_property_trust_estate/resources/estate_planning/an_introduction_to_wills/.

easier as your desires are expressed in the will. Without a will, it is much harder to determine who the executor will be or how to distribute the assets. Once again, The American Bar Association's description is one of the best.[38]

If you don't yet have a will, please create one. It will cost far less in attorney's fees to draw up your will than it will cost in attorney's fees for your loved ones to try and figure (or fight) things out after you die.

Resources:

Keep the Memories, Lose the Stuff by Matt Paxton.

Decluttering Your Home in a Year or Less by Kai M. Jordan.

The Sentimental Person's Guide to Decluttering by Claire Middleton.

Thoreau's Downsizing Planner for Seniors.

https://www.forbes.com/sites/bobcarlson/2019/08/28/wills
-vs-trusts-which-is-best-for-you/?sh=69d5eb7b7abd.

https://www.nerdwallet.com/article/investing/will-vs-trust.

https://www.state.gov/wills-trusts-and-estates/.

https://www.ag.state.mn.us/consumer/handbooks/probate/
CH1.asp.

---

[38] https://www.americanbar.org/groups/real_property_trust_estate/resources/estate_planning/the_probate_process/.

Letter of Intent/Instruction

According to the AARP, a letter of intent is "a flexible, informal supplement to your will that covers more personal information than what is included in your will. You don't need a lawyer to draft a letter of instruction, and you can easily change it as your circumstances or wishes change."[39]

In the letter, it is a good idea to specify that if there is any confusion between what is said in the will or letter of intent, the will prevails. If there are any possibilities that there may be hard feelings when the contents of the will are revealed, the reasons for the disparities should be explained. This can frequently happen when the family is blended or if one member has health issues that may require special support. Sometimes one child has been given money to help with a major purchase earlier, and the parents attempt to "even things out" in the will.

If a friend or family member has taken responsibility for the care of an elderly or ill person, especially if they have not been paid for that care while it was occurring, there may be provisions made in the will to compensate that person. It would be a good idea to explain the reasoning behind this decision in a letter of intent to minimize conflict that may occur.

---

[39] https://www.aarp.org/money/estate-planning/info-04-2009/letter_of_instruction.html.

I have heard letters of intent used to express anger or frustration at family members. I don't recommend this. If something occurs that causes you to decide to leave someone out of your will who would expect to be included, explain your reasoning in as positive or neutral way as possible. Being matter-of-fact, by explaining that because of specific behavior demonstrated by a family member, you have chosen not to include them in the will is better than no explanation and also better than using a demeaning or angry tone. Keep your memory as positive as possible.

Resources:

https://www.nolo.com/legal-encyclopedia/how-write-explanatory-letter-your-will.html.

https://www.agingcare.com/articles/preparing-a-letter-of-instruction-427686.htm.

Before All Is Said and Done by Pat Miles.

Getting Rid of Your Other Stuff

Ideally, you have been working on getting rid of your unused stuff before you go. (See "Shed" chapter.) But just in case you have been caught with your closets brimming, consider adding an addendum to your will and put aside money specifically allocated to dispose of your belongings not wanted by your heirs. My plan is to give my children a year to take what they want from my storage areas, and then I will hire a professional group to sell what is valuable and dispose of the rest.

One way to distribute valuables that are not itemized in your will before the estate sale would be to label them to indicate where you wish them to go. Whatever method you choose, it is important that the family feel that the distribution is done in an equitable manner.

Sometimes there is an item that is particularly valuable and wanted by several heirs. One way to find a resolution is to establish a fair price for the item, hold a lottery to choose who can buy the item, and then add the proceeds from the sale to the estate, to be divided up according to the terms of the will. Nurse Jackie Pederson's family hosts a gathering and dice game to decide who will inherit family heirlooms. Each item is presented (like in an auction). If one person wants the item, their name is attached to it. If more than one person wants an item, they roll dice. The highest number wins. Everything gets recorded, and potential family turmoil is avoided. Get creative to find a system that works for you.

After I die, I will have money put aside in my will to cover the disposal of the belongings that I use up until my death, after my children and extended family have taken what they would like. Frequently one family member, because of their geographic proximity to the deceased, finds themselves responsible for sifting through rooms of "stuff" for months or even years. By delegating this task and providing the funding for a professional to take care of it, you can prevent any dissension or resentment that might arise.

Removal of your unwanted belongings is a growing industry. Check out your local estate sale companies and moving services; many of them are adding disposal services and even apps!

Resources:

Movesforseniors.com

Aligning-spaces.com

https://emptythenest.net/cleanout-service/?gad=1&gclid=
EAIaIQobChMI4-Kzu4mX_wIVzO3jBx0JJQScEAAYAiAAEg-
JrS_D_BwE

https://www.washingtonpost.com/realestate/how-to-handle-
an-estate-liquidation/2016/03/23/780b1ea4-a5d7-11e5-
b53d-972e2751f433_story.html

https://www.mydomaine.com/how-to-organize-your-house-5203629

Thingeology App: Helps preserve stories of treasured possessions and family heirlooms

Healthcare Directives

Please do not consider this legal advice. Always consult with your state laws, and if you move, fill out a new directive that works in your new state.

ADVANCE HEALTHCARE DIRECTIVE

Several weeks before he passed away, my husband Jim decided to enter hospice care. At that time, he worked with his nurse to develop an Advance Healthcare Directive, which would not only ensure his wishes were followed but would also give our children and me the blessing of not having to second-guess our role in his care. When someone you love is dying, it is not unusual to want to do everything possible to keep them alive as long as possible. Hospice care focuses on the quality of life rather than the length of life. Jim's health care directive ensured that he died the way he wanted.

A health care directive allows you to express your wishes in case you cannot express those desires due to injury or illness. It also allows you to appoint a person to make these decisions if you cannot. It is helpful to discuss your wishes with your entire family, to avoid uncomfortable surprises at a stressful time if you become ill.

An advance health care directive is accessible online for every state on https://www.caringinfo.org/planning/advance-directives/ and can be found by searching your state name.

Each state differs in its requirements, but typically a health care directive requires that it be written, include your name, designate an agent to make decisions for you if you cannot, and be signed by witnesses or be notarized.

Advance directives allow you to express your views and values about healthcare in general and the types of medical treatment you would or would not want in specific circumstances. You may also include whether or not you wish to donate your organs.

An advance care directive does not expire, but you should review it periodically. You should also ensure that it is easily accessible to those close to you, as it is only helpful if your healthcare providers have access to it. You can file copies with your hospital and your family, clergy, or friends. There are now digital forms of your directive that can be available on demand, including MedicAlert and even an app on your iPhone or android devices.[40] [41]

DO NOT RESUSCITATE ORDER: DNR

A DNR is a medical order that needs to be signed by a doctor, nurse practitioner, or physician's assistant under the direction of a physician. Laws vary by state, and it is important for you to be aware of the laws in your state and comply with them. Some states have the availability to have a DNR order printed that can be carried in your wallet.

PHYSICIAN'S ORDER FOR LIFE-SUSTAINING TREATMENT: POLST

A POLST would be appropriate if you had a serious illness and needed a DNR (Do Not Resuscitate) order or an order

---

[40] https://apps.apple.com/us/app/mydirectives-mobile/id931433126.

[41] https://www.elderlawanswers.com/advance-medical-directives–now-theres-an-app-for-that-14587.

concerning feeding tubes or mechanical ventilation. A POLST is completed in consultation with your doctor and must be signed by your doctor. These medical orders travel with you and can be used if you need care unexpectedly outside your home area. Most states honor a POLST, but not all. Check the POLST website[42] to see if POLST is honored in your state. Another difference between a POLST and an Advance Care Directive is that a POLST will be honored by an EMT. The difference between a POLST and a DNR order is that a DNR order only covers resuscitation. Typically POLST orders are printed on bright pink paper. They should be posted on the refrigerator or otherwise readily available to the EMTs.

One of the things that I learned about a person in hospice is that the first person to call in an emergency is the hospice nurse. The nurse will contact the EMTs. There is a specific code for hospice that the nurse will give to the EMTs to alert the team that the patient they are caring for is in hospice and, in Jim's case, had a DNR order. If I had called 911 directly without a POLST or DNR order clearly evident when Jim died (either time–see chapter one), the rescuers would have had to perform CPR and try to resuscitate him, even though his entire body was shutting down. The pressure required to provide compressions on a man his age and physical condition would most likely break his ribs or bruise his lungs. If he did survive, he could end up on a ventilator and die in a hospital, which he did not want. By having a clear Health Care Directive in place and working through the hospice system, he died peacefully the way he wanted, at home.

It is critical to note that there are no right or wrong ways to die. Many choose to have everything done to keep them alive as long as possible, and it is wonderful that we have that ability. I

---

[42] https://polst.org/programs-in-your-state/.

am glad my husband made his wishes known and documented so that I would not have to add the guilt of making a wrong decision to the grief of losing him. Thank you, Jim!

Resources:

https://www.caringinfo.org.

https://polst.org/programs-in-your-state/

https://dailycaring.com/the-reality-of-cpr-for-seniors-get-the-facts/.

https://www.nia.nih.gov/health/advance-care-planning-health-care-directives.

https://www.merckmanuals.com/home/fundamentals/legal-and-ethical-issues/do-not-resuscitate-dnr-orders.

Organ Donation

*Don't take your organs to heaven; heaven
knows we need them here.*

—*Maxie Scully*

According to the US government, 106,000 people in the United States are on the National Transplant Waiting List, and seventeen people die each day waiting. It is estimated that one donor can save up to eight lives and enhance seventy-five lives.[43]

I first encountered the miracle of organ donation when I did a Dental General Practice Residency at Loyola University Medical Center in 1985. The heart transplant program was just starting there, and the dental residents rotated through the cardiac program. Before being added to the transplant list, every patient had to be clear of infection, including dental infection. Through the pre-immunosuppressive therapy evaluation we provided for every patient, we had the splendid honor of getting to know them. Every patient, including some children, faced a certain death without the transplant and an uncertain future with the transplant. Because transplants were not yet readily available throughout the country, there was little long-term data on survival. The patients I met faced their destinies with great courage. It was astonishing to see the transformation from

---

[43] https://www.organdonor.gov/learn/organ-donation-statistics.

fatigued, pale, and weak to robust, pink-cheeked, and healthy with the addition of a new heart.

According to the Mayo Clinic, the current (2022) survival rate after a heart transplant is about 90 percent after one year and 80 percent after five years for adults, and approximately 50 percent survive for more than thirteen years. Approximately 75 percent of people live for at least five years after liver transplants.

Those statistics became even more real for me when my husband Jim was diagnosed with liver cancer in 2007. Because a remarkable man from Wisconsin, who was involved in a car accident, had marked "donor" on his license, Jim got a new liver. My daughters and I were able to laugh, cry, have adventures with, and be supported by our husband and father for twelve more years. Jim could see his daughters get married and meet all six of his grandchildren. He loved to point out that he had two sets of DNA, as the donated organ still retained the donor's DNA. He also speculated that if the donated organ were still in good shape when he died, it could be donated again, and theoretically live forever! His doctors told him, however, that they do not transplant an organ more than once.

Typically, solid organ donation can only occur when the patient is in a controlled environment, such as a hospital or an inpatient hospice located within a hospital, where organ recovery can occur at the time of death. Tissues, such as skin, bone, heart valves, and eyes, can be donated up to twenty-four hours following death. Sadly, when Jim died, none of his tissues were acceptable. He had used them all up.

Amy Peele, a former transplant coordinator and current award-winning murder mystery writer, explains, "The most important decision you can make is to let your family and loved ones know if you want to be an organ and tissue donor. Your family will always be asked, but it makes it a lot easier on them if you've already made that decision and communicated it to them."

I am an organ donor, and if I choose hospice for my last days and my organs are healthy enough to donate, I will request a hospice attached to a hospital. The ability to donate is important to me.

Resources:

https://unos.org.

https://www.organdonor.gov.

Hold by Amy Peele.

Match by Amy Peele.

Cut by Amy Peele.

"Cardiac Transplantation: Dental Considerations", K.A. Harms, J.T. Bronny, *Journal of the American Dental Association*, May 1986 https://pubmed.ncbi.nlm.nih.gov/2940281/.

https://www.mayoclinic.org/healthy-lifestyle/consumer-health/in-depth/organ-donation/art-20047529.

Do You Want a Party or a Living Wake?

When I had that miraculous last day with my husband Jim, I called all of his family to let them know that he had weakened tremendously. Those who were in town dropped what they were doing and came to visit. It was a fabulous day and one that I will never forget. Jim was able to say good-bye to everyone either in person or virtually. This was not a planned living wake (more like an impromptu party), but it served the same purpose.

A living wake allows you to say your good-byes. If you are in hospice or suffer a terminal illness, would you like to see those important to you one last time? If so, perhaps you can arrange to throw one last party! It doesn't have to be complicated. You can throw together a simple potluck or go to your favorite restaurant.

A wake is typically an informal time of remembrance and visitation, while a funeral is more formal in nature with rituals and structure.

You can also bring in officiants and have a formal living funeral. Some choose to have a eulogy, a religious ceremony, and a formal good-bye. You can even have your guests sign your coffin or write notes to include in the coffin (which you can read!) The choices are endless.

My daughter, Hillary, promised me that she will throw me a seventieth birthday party in her new house. My life expectancy is currently eighty-six, so I hope to have many years left, but celebrations for significant birthdays are important, especially as we age. For Jim's seventieth birthday in November of 2019, we had planned a trip to Turkey and Greece with our church. Unfortunately, Jim's health would not allow an overseas adventure that required walking. Instead, we went to Universal Studios and rented a motorized cart for Jim. We had a great time. In January 2022, Hillary and I were asked to speak in Hawaii, and we took all of the adults for a fabulous week. A month after that, COVID hit, and we were grounded. By August 2022, Jim was gone. The pictures we have of Jim on his last great adventures are priceless.

My favorite stories of living wake/legacy parties come from my widow's group. When Kathy Dempsy's husband, Ron, found out that his death was imminent, he took the unusual step of saying, "Let's have a party!" Ron's funeral was held before he died. Naomi Rhode tells the tale of her mother-in-law, who insisted on three parties when she turned ninety. She specified to Naomi the details she expected, including ninety attendees at the party to be held at Naomi's house. Naomi complied. I think I will do the same when I turn eighty, just in case I don't make it to ninety. You never know! Hillary, are you reading this?

Death can come suddenly, forgoing the opportunity to plan a living wake. However, if this idea appeals to you, make sure you express your wishes in your legacy folder.

There is never a better time to throw a party than when you are alive!

Resources:
https://en.wikipedia.org/wiki/Living_funeral.

Writing Your Obituary

Obituaries are typically written by a family member or other loved one after we die. It is another obligation we leave for our survivors, which (if they are grieving our loss) can be very difficult. It is hard to think or write clearly when we are suffering.

Why not relieve our survivors of that burden and write an obituary for ourselves, or at least an addendum to the basic obituary format of name, age of death, residence, predeceased, survivors, life summary, and funeral details? You can write your traditional obituary with just the facts or, perhaps, with some elaborations. If you believe you will be going to a "better place," you can even write a humorous and loving letter from the beyond.

My friend, Sheryl Ramstad, shared this obituary addendum (which followed the fact-sharing information part of the obituary) of an attorney friend, Don Weise. I didn't know Don, but after reading this, I hope to meet him in the afterlife. You've got to love this guy! Bravo, Don!

"And Then"

Well, it's over. The end was not so bad and although I can now feel a pull to get on with it here, I can peek in on the funeral before I catch the train for what I think is a ballgame. Nice rainy day down there, not too warm. Not quite the crowd I expected, but then I was pretty old when I finally checked out. All the grandchildren made it, busy as they are. The children and spouses are taking it a bit harder than I wish they would, but they will be okay. And there is Shirley. This is hard for her. When you are an item for five years and then married for way over sixty years, it is hard for one to see down any road that does not include the other. But time will help, and soon we will be together again. The music was great, and no eulogies, thank God. The minister gave the straightforward Christian message, but if they really knew me, it would have been titled "Expectancies Exceeded, Possibilities Virtually Untouched." Lunch was the classic Jell-o® and potato salads, cookies and coffee, short. As I watch this event, something (I don't seem to be totally in control here) is forcing me to think back over my life: all that has happened, all the people I have met, and all the periods of my life, whether I want to remember or not.

I am told about the terrible weather on the 2 of February 1929, the day I was born, when Dad had to shovel all the way from the farmhouse to the main road to get the doctor in; and I remember the cold and heat and the amount of snow that had to be shoveled in the 1930s. I remember the peanut butter sandwiches we had to keep in the cloakroom of the country school lest they freeze solid before our noon lunchtime. I remember high school in LeSueur, my brother going to the Second World War, and my mother and father worrying as they continued to work hard. I remember hunting along the line fence with my best friend. I remember when Shirley and I got together when we were barely seventeen and her putting up with me the rest of the way. I remember attending the University of Minnesota Law School and the subsequent law practice, the work with the Golden Valley school board, the work with the Bar Association, and our house in Golden Valley. I remember all the games as player, coach, and fan, from the LeSueur Farmers to the last grandchild's last game I got to watch. I remember the slow-down years, dodging the bullet for as long as we did, learning how to live with some physical limitations, both Shirley's and mine. I remember the satisfaction I got from watching our children and their spouses and our grandchildren grow up and the unmitigated blessing they always were. Finally, I remember with grateful appreciation all the people with whom we had the good fortune to live, the things large and small that helped us along the way, and for the good luck and proper direction we received. I have the feeling it is time to go. Someone is waiting for me. Perhaps this is when I find out whether all those hours sitting in the church pew are going to pay off. I have a good feeling about it. I saw Jesus warming up his arms a few minutes ago and he said it felt good. After all, if Jesus is pitching for me, what do I really have to worry about? Here comes the train, see you soon.

Best regards and thanks for everything,
Don Wiese

It is clear from reading this that Don loved his family. He used his sense of humor to help soften the grief and remind them that he was okay. Don, you are a role model for me, and I will definitely include an obituary addendum in my legacy folder.

Here is an outline for a fun auto-obituary with an addendum. You can choose to write one or both, or neither!

Obituary:

Name

Age (leave space)

Date of death (with details if appropriate) (leave space)

Where you lived

Family members that predeceased you

Family members that survived you

Life summary

Expressions of your love
Funeral details

Addendum:
Greetings to those left behind
A description of the "better place" you believe you are now. (If you think you may end up in a place that is not "better" than the earth, maybe an auto-obituary is not for you; you don't want to make the grieving worse.)
Fun memories of your life on Earth honoring your loved ones
A loving good-bye
Sign off.

Resources:
https://www.nbcnews.com/better/lifestyle/how-write-per-
    fect-obituary-according-professional-writers-ncna1055996
https://www.joincake.com/blog/how-to-write-an-obituary-for
    -yourself/

Selecting Your Obituary and Memorial Service (Funeral) Pictures

We all want to look good when we are the center of attention, and when will you ever be more the center of attention than at your funeral? I remember that when Jim died, we scoured the pictures of him for hours to find the one we thought represented him best. My daughters and nieces created a beautiful video to play at his service, which took hours to develop.

Why not develop your own video, which you could narrate for astonishing effect, and take that pressure off your loved ones? They can always add to your creation if they find it comforting.

I also have a funeral poster already made with a background featuring the heavenly gates. I physically cut and pasted a picture of Jim, Eric, and I standing in front of the gates with the caption, "Sending you all our love, always, from our heavenly home." I would have included my mother in the group, but I did not have a picture of her that would work. I hope this picture generates some smiles.

What photograph will be selected to represent you as an obituary picture? I have already chosen mine. Jim's sense of adventure inspired it. I had the fantastic opportunity to attend the Eagle Festival in Mongolia with The Delegation for Friendship Among Women. While there, I had the chance to pose on horseback while holding an eagle spreading his wings. I had no makeup, my hair was messy, and the photograph did not capture my good side. I love it!

My children may have chosen a professional headshot with the proper lighting and my hair and makeup just right. But that is not how I want them to remember me. I want to be remembered as "Adventure Grandma." I don't know what the future will bring, and it may hold a time when I am weak, infirm, and with little memory, but at least at my funeral, my grandkids will remember that their Nana once sat on a horse, holding an eagle in the mountains surrounding the Gobi Desert!

Do you have a favorite obituary picture? If not, go create one!

Resources:

https://www.joincake.com/blog/obituary-photo/

https://www.hrrv.org/blog/gift-ideas-for-hospice-patients/

Where Will My Remains Remain?

When I was young, the only type of burial I was familiar with was a traditional burial where the body was embalmed; we had a viewing and then burial in a local cemetery. The first crematories were built in Europe and the United States in the late 1800s, but numerous cultures have been burning dead bodies since the Stone Age.

Today, there are even more options:

Traditional burial (religious or humanist) has changed over time. Years ago, the family typically took care of the body and frequently buried it in a simple wooden coffin in a local or family cemetery. More recently, funeral directors manage the care of the body and memorial services. I have to say that I have appreciated this care by the White Family Funeral Homes for my son's burial and my husband's cremation. Eric was buried, and Jim's cremated remains are buried at Ft. Snelling National Cemetery. I plan to have my cremated remains buried in the same spot.

A special workshop in Ghana makes colorful works of art as coffins. Patrons of the workshop bury their dead in fanciful coffins shaped like fish, animals, pencils, or other objects that represent something important to the deceased.

Mausoleums are above-ground structures designed to hold a casket in the place of burial underground. Columbariums are above-ground structures designed to hold cremation urns.

Cremation is growing in popularity. Cremated remains can be buried or spread out in certain areas. After Eric died, I met with a remarkable group of women who had lost their children to suicide. One of the Eric Harms Libraries is dedicated to the memory of all of our sons. The ashes of three of the boys nurture a beautiful hibiscus tree and a mountainside near the library. Hindu funerals include a cremation ceremony followed by a ceremony to help the deceased's spirit enter the next world.

Burial at sea involves the disposal of the deceased into the ocean either by ship or aircraft. Cremated remains can also be disposed of in this way. Another type of burial at sea involves using the deceased's ashes to form an artificial reef by mixing the ashes with concrete before dropping the block into the ocean.

Natural or green burial is defined by the Green Burial Council[44] as "a way of caring for the dead with the minimal environmental impact that aids in the conservation of natural resources, (and strives for) reduction of carbon emissions, protection of worker health, and the restoration or preservation of habitat. Green burial uses all biodegradable materials and does not involve embalming. A number of guidelines must be followed for a natural burial. If you are interested, check with individual state law and look for natural burial grounds, cemeteries, or preserves in your area.

Composted burial involves putting the body in a container and mixing it with straw and other organic materials to compost it. The process typically takes about thirty days. Make sure you are working with a funeral service that is fully licensed for composting and that composting bodies are a legal alternative in your state.

Diamond burials are also on the rise. Our bodies and diamonds are both made from carbon. Diamond burials involve

---

[44] https://www.greenburialcouncil.org.

taking the carbon from our bodies and hair and subjecting it to extremely high pressure and temperature, and then, *voila, we* are a diamond. Make sure you do your homework, select a reputable company, and follow all state laws.

Cryonics is the freezing and storage of human bodies. Many hope that the bodies can be unfrozen at a time the disease they died from has a cure. As far as I know, no human bodies have been unfrozen and revived yet.

Aquamation uses water and alkalinity to break down the body. It is then returned to the family as ash. Aquamation is considered eco-friendly as it uses significantly less energy than cremation.

Donating your body to science is one way to help humanity after you die. Donated bodies are used to train medical personnel and assist in research. It is also a donation, which means free!

Space burial (or really the spreading of a memorial portion of your cremated remains) is now possible. A number of companies offer this unique service. You can have your remains shot into space, orbit the earth, and return as a "shooting star," land on the moon, or travel into the depths of the Milky Way.

Memorial art takes your cremated remains and works them into an artwork either directly or provides a special place in the artwork for the ashes.

Sky burial is typically illegal in the United States but practiced in some areas, including Tibet and Mongolia. With this practice, bodies are left on a mountaintop or hillside to decompose or be eaten by scavengers.

Resources:
https://funerals.org/?consumers=earth-burial-tradition-sim-
plicity.
https://cremationinstitute.com/cremation-process/.

https://cryonics.org.

https://aquamationinfo.com.

https://www.mayoclinic.org/body-donation/making-donation.

https://pages.celestis.com/memorial.

https://beyondburials.com.

https://www.spiritpieces.com/collections/top-seller-memorial-art.

What Do You Want on Your Tombstone?

When someone dies, especially if they die suddenly, it may be hard to find the right words to memorialize them on their headstone. When Eric died, we were so overcome with grief that all we could come up with was Beloved Son and Beloved Brother. We were better prepared when Jim passed away, and since he was cremated, we had more time before the actual burial at Ft. Snelling. We used our favorite Jim quote: "Life is an adventure!"

Writing your epitaph may serve as a tribute to you from your loved ones, and it may be appropriate to allow them to write it. However, if you want to save them the trouble, make sure you leave specific instructions in your legacy folder. Epitaphs typically include:

Your full name

Birth and death dates (death date to be filled out later)

A phrase or two that will represent you to those viewing your headstone.

Also, check to ensure the epitaph is acceptable for the cemetery you choose. There may be some limitations as to what is appropriate at specific sites, and you don't want to put any additional stress on your survivors if your wishes cannot be honored or, worse yet, you have the additional expense of re-preparing the headstone.

Years ago, I was at a school board retreat, and we were asked to write our epitaph. I wrote, "She may be gone, but her fillings live on!" (This refers to my job as a dentist.) Recently a friend and fellow dentist, Dr. Michael O'Brien, shared his epitaph with me. "Dr. Michael O'Brien: in the Largest Cavity He Has Ever Filled." We, dentists, have a good sense of humor!

Although some epitaphs will reflect the person's profession, especially if that person is a poet, writer, or musician, most will reflect a deeper part of the person's character. Some are witty, some are funny, and some reflect the loss experienced by those who loved them. Here are some of my favorites:

Martin Luther King Jr.: "*Free at Last, Free at Last, Thank God Almighty I'm Free at Last.*"

Coretta Scott King: "*And now abide Faith, Hope, Love, These Three: But the greatest of these is Love. I Cor. 13:13.*"

Winston Churchill: (Churchill wrote this himself fifteen years before he died.) "*I am ready to meet my Maker. Whether my Maker is prepared for the great ordeal of meeting me is another matter.*"

George Burns and Gracie Allen were one of the finest comedy duos in history. They were also deeply in love. Their tombstone reads: "*Together Again.*"

Lester Moore (Wells Fargo clerk): "*HERE LIES LESTER MOORE, FOUR SLUGS FROM A .44, NO LES NO MORE.*"

If you choose to have a memorial headstone, what would you like it to say? As we age, our preferences may change. At this time, I would like to share an epitaph with Coretta Scott King. I believe passages from the Bible are fair game!

Funeral Planning: Acknowledging Your Appointment with Death

Do you want a funeral? If the answer is no, make sure you have expressed that in writing and hopefully have discussed this with your survivors. Ensure your executor is given clear direction on making your wishes known. If you want a funeral, discuss the arrangements with your family and document your wishes. It is hard to plan anything while in the throes of grief.

___ Whom would you like to handle your funeral?

___ Where would you like your funeral to be held?

___ Pick out your memorial/obituary photo.

___ Write your obituary or give information to someone else to write it.

___ Do you want your death to be announced on social media?

___ Whom do you want to be contacted after you die?

___ Do you have an email or phone list of people you would like notified?

___ Express your view on viewings.

___ Make sure you designate the person in charge of your funeral in writing.

___ What is going to happen to your body after you die? Burial, cremation, donation, etc.!

___ What is your funeral budget?

___ Have you talked with your loved ones to determine how you will be buried?

___ Special Music

___ Picture board and DVD

___ Would you like to make a personal "good-bye" video?

___ Have you told your life story to ensure all the details are correct? A life video or story written in advance will help get the facts right.

___ Whom would you like to officiate the service?

___ Religious preferences?

___ Would you like a virtual or hybrid event?

_____

_____

_____

_____

_____

_____

_____

_____

_____

_____

Funeral Recipes

Look back on your life and remember a favorite aunt, grandmother, or uncle. Did they make you something special when you visited? My Great Aunt Nonie and Uncle Henry would give us a bottle of Coke and a cookie every time we visited. Today, that may not seem like such a memorable treat, but in those days, we were not allowed soft drinks regularly, and homemade cookies were a rarity. Fifty years after their passing, I still associate Aunt Nonie and Uncle Henry with love, a Coke, and a cookie.

Carol Johnson was my best friend as our children grew. We saw each other through some very difficult times. The week after giving my daughter, Ashley's, wedding shower, Carol was diagnosed with terminal gallbladder cancer. Through the first months after her diagnosis, she continued to work as a nurse for our local obstetrics group, and the last babies she helped deliver were our twin granddaughters, Anna and Lily.

Carol was an amazing cook and baker known for her wonderful whoopie pies. Carol gave me her recipe to publish and distribute at her funeral. They were very well received. Making her whoopie pies brings her memory back for those who loved her.

Do you have a favorite recipe you can give your loved ones? Do you have a recipe that your funeral attendees would appreciate? In memory of my friend, Carol, here is the recipe we handed out at her funeral.

CAROL'S FAMOUS WHOOPIE PIES

Cookie:
1 cup butter softened
1-1/2 cup sugar
2 eggs
2 tsp. vanilla extract
4 cups all-purpose flour
3/4 cup baking cocoa
2 tsp. baking soda
1/2 tsp. salt
1 cup water
1 cup buttermilk
Cream butter and sugar.
Add eggs and vanilla, mix well.
In a different bowl, combine flour, cocoa, baking soda, and salt.
Add to creamed mixture alternatively with buttermilk and water.
Drop by teaspoonful two inches apart on greased baking sheet.
Bake 375°F for five-seven minutes until set.

Filling:
1/4 cup hot water
3 cups powdered sugar
1 stick butter-flavored Crisco
Vanilla and butter extract to taste
Beat hot water and powdered sugar until smooth. Add Crisco and flavorings and beat for ten minutes on high.
Sandwich filling between two cookies (makes three dozen) and enjoy!

Memorial Playlist

One of the things that personalizes us is the music we love. My husband Jim used to play the guitar, and his nieces and nephews fondly remember dancing at our wedding to Jim playing the song "Proud Mary" by John Fogarty. Every time we heard Creedence Clearwater Revival play that song on the radio, our thoughts were transported back to the beautiful day we were married in Missouri.

According to *Psychology Today*, music can transport us back in time and evokes powerful emotions. This is especially true when a sentimental event and a piece of music are tied together.[45]

My mother-in-law, Inez, wanted the last song at her funeral to be "I'll Fly Away" by Albert Brumley. That has become the family's go-to last funeral song, and we played it at Jim's. Every time we hear or sing that song, we think of our loved ones who have passed away.

I spend much time with my Minnesota grandchildren in the car, and we have a playlist. The stipulations for song inclusion are that they are positive and have no swear words. Each of us picks out our favorite songs that meet those requirements. My songs include secular pieces (typically by The Moody Blues, Queen, or The Beatles) and my favorite sacred pieces. Jim loved an unusual song written by a Jewish man, Norman Greenbaum,

[45] Shahram Heshmat Ph.D., psychologytoday.com, September 14, 2021.

about his thoughts on Christianity. "Spirit in the Sky" was not exactly theologically correct, especially the verse about never being a sinner (Christians believe we are all sinners). Still, it is a great song, and every time we hear it, we say, "This is Pop Pop's song." Tying our favorite music to us (especially if it is upbeat) will help keep our memory alive even after we are gone.

Consider developing a funeral playlist of music you would like to represent you at your memorial service. Better yet, consider creating a playlist for your family to play with you while you are still physically present in their lives. The memories you develop will be priceless.

Resources:

https://www.nytimes.com/2020/04/10/smarter-living/make-the-perfect-playlist-spotify-apple-music-pandora.html

https://tonedeaf.thebrag.com/how-to-make-the-perfect-playlist-a-step-by-step-guide/

Death Prepper's Emotional Life Insurance Plan

We all know the importance of life insurance to make sure our loved ones are financially secure after we die, but what can we do to help insure they are emotionally secure without us? The best thing you can do for those you love is to build your relationships NOW! Life can get in the way, and our children (along with our grandchildren) frequently move to other parts of the country or even other parts of the world. Fortunately, we can keep in touch electronically. When my grandchildren got their first phones, I made a point to send them an almost daily text with an "I love you" theme. Sometimes it is a cute picture of their early life; sometimes it is a corny joke, riddle, or saying, and sometimes, it is just a cluster of hearts. The point is that they know I love them and am thinking about them every day. What can you do to build your relationships now?

As we prepare for the future and a time when we will not be physically present to build relationships, here are some tasks you can accomplish to remind your loved ones that you did, indeed, love them. Some you can include in your legacy folder to be opened after your death, but some you can send out now.

___acknowledge Tasks of Mourning (see next chapter): Acceptance, Processing, Adjusting, New Life

___write Legacy Love Letters to loved ones. These can always be updated!

___apologize to those whom you have hurt

___ reconcile to build back relationships

___ give family history

___ discuss family medical history

___ offer favorite recipes

___ pass along keepsakes

___ have old family videos preserved

___ make a "This Is My Life" family history video

___ make my favorite memories of each loved one video

___ make a good-bye video

___ share videos or put videos on a flash drive

___ document video information in a homemade book

___ make a "This Is My Life" book from your pictures

___ document family traits shared by relatives

___ make a gratitude journal or write gratitude cards

___ create birthday, holiday, and Valentine cards to deliver after you are gone

___ purchase and wrap the first Christmas/birthday gift for the first year after you are gone

___ write a letter to be delivered to your loved ones at graduation, wedding, the birth of your first child, and other important events. You can hand them out yourself if you are alive and they will be even more treasured if received after you have passed on.

Additional ideas:

_____

_____

_____

_____

_____

_____ Resources:

(For Children): *The Invisible String*, Patrice Karst, Little Brown and Company, Boston, 2000/2018.

Naomi and the Widow's Club: A Safe Strong Place After the Loss of a Spouse, Naomi Rhode and Kim Harms, Muse Publishing, Chicago 2022.

Tell Me Your Story Mom, Questions about Me, 2021.

I Wrote a Book About You, M.H. Clark, Compendium Inc. 2016, Seattle.

Letters to My Dad in Heaven, Made in the United States, Orlando, Florida, 2022.

God Gave Us Heaven, Lisa Tawn Bergen, WaterBrook and imprint of Crown Publishing, a division of Penguin Random House L.L.C., New York, 2008.

The Memory Box; A Book About Grief, Joanna Rowland, The Sparkhouse Family, Minneapolis, 2017.

Grandparents Legacy Journal, Memory Book: Family Tree Keepsake by Duncan and Stone.

The Tasks of Mourning

One of the things we can't control when we die is that our loss will leave an emotional void in the lives of the people we love. We can't fix this, but we need to understand grief and help our loved ones understand it.

A year after my son, Eric, died, I developed irreversible nerve damage to my dental "drilling fingers" and was told by the doctors at Mayo Clinic that I would have to look for another career. In just two and a half years, I had lost my role as a sister and mother. I had come close to losing my role as a wife. Now my clinical career as a dentist was over. What the heck!

I was deep in the depths of that hellish despair pit, and it seemed that any progress I made in the upward direction was soon countered by another punch down. I desperately needed a grief counselor but was too proud to seek one. So, since I now had time on my hands, I thought I would become one. I spent the next several months studying hard to get certified as a grief counselor. My career in grief counseling, however, was short-lived. Although I think I was of help to those I served, I was left exhausted. I was not yet healed enough of my own grief to help others.

One of the most important discoveries of my grief counselor journey was that there were tasks to mourning. Tasks! My concrete dentist brain loves tasks. Sure, grief has stages (Kubler-Ross), but mourning has tasks (psychologist J. William Worden)! Stages are indefinite, but tasks can be completed.

I love tasks!

Grief and mourning are different things. Grief is the personal experience of a loss, and mourning is the process that occurs after the loss. After you die, your loved ones will mourn your loss. By understanding these tasks, you will better know what they will be going through and, therefore, better understand what you can do now to make these tasks easier for them later.

The first task of mourning is to accept the reality of the loss. This may seem simple, but when something catastrophic occurs, like the death of a loved one, it is sometimes difficult for the mind to adjust. Having those end-of-life and legacy discussions may help your loved ones work through this task.

Task number two is processing the pain of the loss. This is the toughest task, in my opinion. Processing the pain is, well, *painful*, and the more you love someone, the more difficult it is to process their loss. Interestingly, broken relationships can be extremely difficult to work through as shame and guilt are frequently added to the mix of emotions. By reconciling with your loved ones, you may help them through this task.

The third task of mourning is adjusting to the world that exists after the loss. Widows and widowers frequently have difficulty managing household responsibilities that their spouses always managed. Helping your loved ones become independent by teaching them those responsibilities and leaving your passwords, financial information, etc., available to them (see "Death Prepper's Goal Setting Guide") will help them complete task number three.

The fourth and final task of mourning is to develop a lasting connection to your loss that does not interfere with the process of embarking on your new life. This task involves living your present life without letting your past life interfere. It is a difficult task for most but very important.

Our loved ones may experience survivor's guilt, especially if our death is outside the expected sequence. We want our loved ones to continue on and be happy and joyful in their lives even when we are not there to share it. My husband, Jim, was an extreme extrovert. We knew that if I died first, he would need to find another wife. We even included that thought in our estate planning. We can help our family through this task by telling them that our most important wish is that they are happy while we are here and that they work through their grief to find happiness when we are gone.

When I write my legacy letters to my loved ones, I am going to include a section on the tasks of mourning with helpful hints as to how they can work through those tasks and get to the point where their memory of me brings them happiness and not sadness

Resources:

https://www.va.gov/WHOLEHEALTHLIBRARY/tools/grief-reactions-duration-and-tasks-of-mourning.asp

https://www.therapistaid.com/therapy-worksheet/tasks-of-mourning

https://www.youtube.com/watch?v=QRrDHjmjzVg

Documenting Your Family History

Several months before my husband died, our daughter, Ashley, recorded his history in a video to submit to a company that would make the recording into a book. Unfortunately, that company went out of business. Fortunately for us, Ashley saved a copy of the video, transcribed it herself, tracked down several old pictures, and made her own book using a conventional, Internet printing service. It is a masterful display of love and a priceless family treasure.

My friend, Kim Miles, who lost two sons, showed me a book made by her son David's coworkers. David died suddenly of an aneurysm, a shock to all. His work team made a memory book filled with pictures taken over the years of his life at work. It was made digitally and then published into a book by an online printing company. What a thoughtful and comforting gift!

We also have a video of Jim's mother, Inez, discussing her childhood in the Saskatchewan prairie. In it, she describes riding in a sled to the small village schoolhouse with hot potatoes in her pockets to keep her hands warm and, later, to eat for lunch. She describes eloping in the next town with Jim's father, Sam, during the Depression. A few years later, she bemoaned the fact that she had not yet had a child to her sisters. They recommended that Inez take a bottle of Lydia Pinkham's Elixir with "A baby in every bottle" proudly proclaimed on its label. In the next seventeen years, Inez had fourteen children. By the time Jim, number twelve, was born, the family had run out of names. The Harms children were delivered at home, and the older brothers and sisters had been lined up on the steps awaiting the first cry of their new sibling. Apparently, after a discussion on the stairwell, Jim was at least partially named after a boy one of his sisters had a crush on.

It is interesting to note that it is not always the major life accomplishments but the everyday stories we find the most interesting. Don't worry if you haven't won a Pulitzer Prize or been nominated for an Academy Award; the simple things are the most interesting when measuring your life and telling your story. If you have some funny stories about decisions you made in life, tell those. Also, stories of hardship help your survivors understand who you are and the circumstances that shaped you. Talk about how you met the people you love, about your parents, and about important lessons you learned. If you have a family history that has not been documented, this is a good time to tell the story. This is also a good time to discuss your religious and personal philosophy and your hopes for the future.

Jim's sister, Sonja, would send a "family tree" composition to all the nieces and nephews when they graduated from high school. It would include pictures of their great-grandparents, grandparents, parents, and the graduate pictured as the trunk. With commercial genealogical services, making a family tree is easier than ever and can open up a number of discussions. If possible, sharing the family's medical history can also be valuable to future generations and shared with their healthcare team.

When each of my children graduated from high school, they got a scrapbook carefully made of printed photographs and festooned with ribbons, cut-outs, stickers, and stamps. It took me many hours to assemble each page, but my children knew that these memories were precious to me and each book was a labor of love from their mother. For my legacy project, I am assembling a small "Adventures with NaNa" booklet for each of my grandchildren. They are filled with affirming thoughts and pictures of various escapades we share. Of course, as I work to construct these pages, I am motivated to seek out even more adventures! Depending on how old I get, I may need to make more adventure books!

Transferring old family videos into digital form is another way to share family history. There are many companies available that will do this for you. Some will even work with you to develop a composite video that can be shown at family gatherings or used for a memorial service. The day before Jim died, his brother showed us all a fifty-year-old video of the brothers climbing Mt Whitney. Not only did Jim enjoy looking back on his youth, but his children were also able to see what an adventurer their dad was. The miracle of digitalization allows your memories to be shared with family and friends worldwide with just a touch on your phone and can be very comforting, especially during times of loss.

At a recent family wedding my niece Becky commented that her Aunties resembled those in a popular commercial. This prompted us to make our own short video *Invasion of the Norwegian Aunties* that we put on YouTube. It was a family hit and memorialized a moment in time when we elderly aunties could laugh at our idiosyncrasies.

However you plan to share your legacy, the best time to start is now!

The first thing to do is to make a plan. The following questionnaire is designed to help you decide what is important to you, what you want to share, how you want to share, and who you want to share it with!

Resources
Legacyletters.org.

Legacy Questionnaire: Organizing Your Thoughts

Name: _____

Please describe the important people in your life who have passed away:

_____

_____

_____

_____

_____

What could they have said or done before they died that would have made your grief journey after they died a bit easier?

_____

_____

_____

_____

_____

Who are the people you expect to survive you? (Please include any loved one alive; you never know who will go first!)

_____

_____

_____

_____

What can you share with them to let them know they are loved and help them with their grief journey?

_____

_____

_____

_____

_____

Do you have any examples (can be expressed anonymously) where a family member or friend failed to work out a plan for their family's financial or emotional survival? What were the consequences?

_____

_____

_____

_____

_____

What do you believe will happen to you when you die? Are there some encouraging images that you can describe for your family?

_____

_____

_____

_____

_____

Do you have any unusual stories surrounding the death of a family member or friend?

_____

_____

_____

_____

What goals would you like to accomplish before you die (your bucket list)? How many of these goals involve showing the important people in your life how much you love them?

_____
_____
_____
_____
_____

Do you have any fears about your future? Do you fear death?

_____
_____
_____
_____
_____

Who would benefit from a legacy letter written by you to be given to them after you pass away?

_____
_____
_____
_____
_____

Name them:

_____
_____
_____
_____
_____

Do you need to apologize to anyone? Name them:

_____

_____

_____

_____

_____

Who are the people in your life that made a positive difference? Would they benefit by hearing from you how grateful you are? Name them:

_____

_____

_____

_____

_____

From your list above, which five names would you consider the most important?

_____

_____

_____

_____

_____

If you write five letters today (you can always update and expand) and five letters next week, how long will it take you to write letters to everyone on your list? _____

How many letters can I get done today? _____?

GET STARTED. THE SOONER, THE BETTER!

Video Interviews or Legacy Document Proposed Questions

Choose those that you want to answer, then have a friend record you on your phone or another recording device. (Zoom works great). You can also do this on your own by simply picking out the questions you want to answer as well as any you would like to add and record away! Send this recording to a loved one who can keep it. You can also put the recording on a memory stick or DVD and place it in your legacy folder/binder. My favorite recommendation is to share this video on social media for the entire family while you are still around so that they can ask questions and engage in the stories!

Here are some proposed questions, pick out the ones you like and feel free to add your own:

Where were you born?

Tell me about your parents and grandparents.

Tell the story about how your grandparents and parents met.

If you are married, how did you meet your spouse?

How would you describe your early life? What technology did you NOT have, and how did you cope?

Describe the house (houses) and the neighborhood you grew up in.

What historical events do you remember, and how did they affect your life?

Did your ancestors live through historically difficult times? How did they manage?

What was the biggest lesson you learned from work?

What was your most embarrassing moment?

Please tell as many funny stories about your life as you can! Are there any family jokes that have been passed down through the generations?

What is a favorite memory of your: grandparents, parents, children, grandchildren, important people, special friends, or others? Who were your best friends, and what did they teach you?

What was your birth order? Did your birth order have an effect on your life?

Describe your best friends. What is the secret to friendship? What did you have in common?

Did you have a bad relationship with a friend? If so, what did you learn from it!

What is your favorite food? Please share a favorite recipe.

What challenges did you overcome?

What is the most important lesson you learned in your life?

Describe the day your children, grandchildren, or other important people in your life were born.

What are you grateful for? What are you grateful for about the special people in your life?

What have been the most important lessons you learned from life?

What music would be on your favorite playlist?

What is your favorite book and why?

What is your favorite movie and why?

Are there any special phrases, expressions, or sayings important to your family?

What is the best piece of advice you have received in your life?

What advice would you give to your children or grandchildren
when they reach:
- their teenage years
- their twenties
- their thirties
- their forties
- their fifties, sixties, seventies, eighties, and beyond.

If your loved ones get married, what is your advice for a good
marriage?

Describe an event or time in your life that would be a surprise
for your survivors.

What jobs did you have?

Do you have traits that have been passed down through the
generations?

Do you have any bad habits you would like to break?

What was your greatest adventure?

Do you have any important parenting advice?

What have you done in your life to encourage relationships?

When your loved ones graduate, what is your advice for them?

Did you have any mentors? What did they do for you?

Describe your wishes for the future for the important people in
your life.

What are the greatest accomplishments in your life?

What are the most important characteristics of a "good life"?

What are your religious beliefs?

What do you believe will happen to you when you die?

How would you like to be remembered?

What do you want your legacy to be?

Additional Questions:

_____

_____

_____

_____

_____

_____

Legacy Books Focused on One Particular Person

I made this book for you because _____.

I love it when you _____.

My favorite memory of our time together was _____.

You are a brilliant _____.

You make me laugh when you _____.

Do you remember when _____?

You are exceptionally talented at _____.

My hope for your future is _____.

I love to watch you _____.

My most important message to you is_____.

I love you!

I am proud of you!

The Grateful but Not Yet Dead Tour

My dear friend and partner in legacy building, Terri Hands, came up with a unique way to show her gratitude. She gathered old photos of her high school days and brought them with her to her high school class reunion. Imagine the gaiety and happiness those pictures brought to the recipients. Do you have a special place to visit and special people to express your gratitude to?

After I lost my ability to practice dentistry, I planned my own grateful but not yet dead tours. My first was to my mother's hometown, Cincinnati, Ohio, to visit her only living brother, my Uncle Tom, and his family. Tom was the last living uncle, and he played a big role in my life when we lived with my mother. He was now extremely ill and in hospice at home. His hospital bed was placed prominently in the living room, a clear indication that he did not want to miss anything going on in his home. His wife, my still red-headed Aunt Ruth, although frail herself, took loving care of him. If he needed to be lifted or bathed, his sons showed up.

When I told my uncle who I was (it had been about forty years since he had last seen me), he started to cry. I was able to tell Tom how grateful I was for the time and attention he paid to me as a child and his inclusion of my brother and sister and me in his family activities. I described specific events, including learning to swim in his swimming pool and crashing my bike at the bottom of the hill in front of his house. I was also able to thank Aunt Ruth for her wonderful cooking and fun-loving personality.

My second trip was to my last living uncle on my father's side of the family. Uncle Jack and Aunt Hazel were wonderful. They told me tales of my father, and their love for my mother and gave me pictures and mementos of my grandparents. During these sojourns, I had life-affirming discussions, collected new stories and new photographs of my early life, and brought love and comfort to my aging uncles and aunts.

My friend from fourth grade, Nancy, called me recently and planned a grade school reunion in her new hometown of Lewis, Delaware. It was fabulous!. Even after fifty years and a wide range of career choices, we all reverted to our fourth-grade selves and had a wonderful time together. Our next gathering will be in the Northwoods of Minnesota!

Are there aging aunts or uncles or others in your life you would like to thank? Do you have younger friends or relatives who need to know how much you love them? Are you anxious to reconnect with a special group of friends?

Tips for planning your own Grateful But Not Yet Dead Tour:

1. Decide which group(s) you would like to reconnect with (friends, family, classmates).
2. Make a list of the special people in this group.
3. Is there a convenient meeting place that would be appropriate for the group?
4. Would your group fit best at a hotel, vacation home, or family home?
5. Is there a "leader" in this group who would like to plan this event?
6. Do you have pictures or other mementos that you could bring to the gathering?

7. Could you write a letter or list of the reasons you are grateful for these people?
8. What legacies can you bring to leave with this special group?

Resources:

https://www.cancer.org/cancer/end-of-life-care/nearing-the-end-of-life/saying-goodbye.html

https://www.theglobeandmail.com/life/first-person/article-ive-decided-on-a-goodbye-tour-not-a-bucket-list-trip/

Legacy Letters and Legacy Love Letters:

One of the simplest ways of sharing your legacy is to write a letter. A legacy letter, like a legacy video or book, is used to tell your story and your family's story. A legacy love letter tells your survivors how much you love or care about them and any wisdom you would like to pass along. There are no rules to writing these letters, but I will share some ideas to help you get started.

One of the oldest legacy love letters I know of was written by St. Valentine. Legend has it that he wrote to a young girl, Julia, whom he had cured of blindness. In the letter, St. Valentine encouraged her and let her know he would always be with her and would be present in her heart forever. This legacy love letter was his last act before being brought to his execution under Roman Emperor Claudius II. Julia must have appreciated the gesture, as legend also has it that she planted a beautiful almond tree above Valentine's grave.

You may want to write one legacy letter/video/book for your entire family and then personal legacy love letters for each family member.

As you write your legacy letters, keep them positive by thinking of the good they will do. This is not the time to be critical or to bring up past grievances. Write with love and the hope that what you say will be of great benefit to the recipient of the letter. Jeremy Brown writes in his book, *The Necessity of Legacy: Why Your Story Is Needed and How To Make It Last,* "Family legacy *gives us confidence. Their words give us direction, comfort, and clarity. Sometimes, we just need to know the words. We need to hear them, and we need to feel them."*

"We are simply asking our patriarchs and matriarchs to be bold in their declarations. To be honest in their storytelling and to speak loving words to the generations that will proceed with them. Because their legacy is a priceless gift. Their memories, their beliefs, their values, and their history mean everything for all of us in years to come... Legacy gives us affirmation and it matters."

One of my closest friends described a letter written to her son when he was born. It was from her father. She wants to remain anonymous, so we will just use the first names here. It was meant to be opened when her son was eighteen years old.

My Dear, Dear John,

You were born two days ago.

I called your father and felt so completely happy that you had come into this world. I also felt so proud of your mother... and how she has handled your pregnancy. I had gone to mass at St. Francis Chapel on the ground floor of the Prudential Building [in Boston]. My prayer that day was for you and your mother. The next day I went again.

I know your brother Joe wanted a brother. When we visited... at Easter, Joe had a new outfit of clothes, and he said he wanted to dress like a big brother.

I called Grandma Ellen tonight. She said you were (are) beautiful. Joe and Larry were getting a new baseball uniform and having a picture taken.

So, John, I'm thrilled you are here. I will be working to see you have a decent world to inhabit if we have not solved poverty, pollution, torture, racism, and hate, and if there ain't enough love, to do something about it.

I love you,

Grandpa John.

I love this letter. Grandpa John wrote a letter to welcome his grandson at birth, and Don Weise wrote a letter (obituary) to say good-bye! What kind of letter can you create for those you love?

Sample Template for Legacy Love Letter
Dear _____,

I am so grateful (blessed, thankful, happy) to have had you in my life. (Then describe why and extoll their good virtues.)

When I look back on our (my) family, the most important things I learned were _____. My Faith has taught me _____What matters most to me is _____. My hope for you is _____.

Thank you again for all that you brought into my life.

With all my love,

Mom (Grandma, Dad, Grandpa, Name)

Optional Script on the Tasks of Mourning
Please adjust and adapt as you see fit and customize it. The intent is to bring comfort.

My dear _____,

Psychologist J. William Worden described four tasks that help us understand how we journey through grief. He described them as the Four Tasks

261

of Mourning. Everyone proceeds through these tasks in different ways and at different times. Everyone's journey is unique. I hope that your voyage through these tasks is short and that you will remember me with happiness in your heart, not sadness.

Task Number One: Accept the Reality of the Loss
When I am gone, it may take some time to realize that (describe something that you do on a regular basis), I am not physically present to participate in the things we shared. (Describe holidays, events, or favorite subjects you had in common.) Although I am no longer there in the flesh, please know that my spirit and love will always be with you.

Task Number Two: Process the Pain
I believe this is typically the hardest task. Grief is painful. The brain processes it as a traumatic experience. Processing that pain may take weeks or months or years. Everyone manages differently. Please work hard on this task and fight through the grief as hard as possible. You may feel sometimes that you have conquered it, but a date on the calendar, a memory, or an event can strike you right back down again. If it does, battle again to get back up!

Task Number Three: Adjust to Your New World
When someone dies, your own identity changes in that you no longer have that relationship in a physical sense. I hope I have prepared you well for a time without me, but please strive to adapt to the void I leave. You may need to learn to (manage the finances, take out the trash, or teach the grandkids how to fish). Please know and understand that you are enough even if you are alone.

Task Number Four: Find a New Life With an Enduring Connection
I want you to be happy, and the best way you can honor my life is to live yours with happiness and joy. One of my main missions in life is to help

my loved ones become kind, caring, compassionate, and joyful people, no matter their circumstances. Your joy brings honor to my life. Work for it.

With much (love, affection, respect etc.)

(Your name in familiar, loving terms, Mom, Dad, Grandpa......))

Template for Letter to be Given at Important Events:

The most important part of this type of letter is to be loving and sincere. Use personal anecdotes whenever possible! Keep it unique to your relationship!

Dear _____,

Congratulations on this special day. (Specify graduation, wedding, birthday.)
I am so proud of you. (Specify again.)
I remember when_____.
My hope for you is _____.
The best advice I can give you is_____.
Please know how much I love you!

Mom, Dad, Grandma, or Grandpa

Words of Wisdom and Legacy Questions for Legacy Letters and Love Letters:

    important things you learned in your life
    people who mattered
    special words for each person
    What makes them unique?
    special advice for their future
    your hopes for them

faith

failure

success

education

What can they learn from historical conflicts?

raising a family

cultural lessons

favorite moments to cherish and promote in the future

vacation

family

work

lessons for raising a family

special talents or hobbies

general advice.

Resources:

https://www.legacyletter.org

https://www.legacyletterchallenge.com/home

https://www.barnesandnoble.com/w/
    the-legacy-letters-carrie-lloyd/1140831346

https://www.joincake.com/blog/legacy-letters/

Reconciliation Letters

*Reconciliation and forgiveness can actually help
all of us move on in a healthier, happier way.*
—*Chesa Boudin*

Is there someone important in your life that you are estranged
from and whose relationship you miss? Is that person deserving of a second chance? Would contacting that person be a
healthy choice for you? If so, perhaps you should consider a
reconciliation letter.

Reconciliation (according to the Oxford dictionary) is the
restoration of friendly relations. Forgiveness and grace are necessary to reconcile.

There is no need to establish who was right and wrong, even
if you feel right. If you were wrong, then an apology would be a
good way to start a reconciliation. You are the one initiating an
attempt to reconcile, and the best way to do that is to show grace
to the other person.

As a Christian, I believe that Jesus died on the cross to reconcile
me with God, and therefore, I must do my part to reconcile with
my brothers and sisters (that means everybody) here on Earth.

Other religions also teach the importance of reconciliation,
and even those who do not profess religious beliefs understand
the importance of working toward harmony among their fellow
humans.

The difference between a reconciliation letter and an apology letter is that a reconciliation letter does not have to admit blame. Neither letter should assign blame to anyone else. A reconciliation letter should focus on rebuilding the relationship. The goal is harmony.

So what are the steps to reconcile? The first step is ensuring you are adequately motivated to seek reconciliation. The best motivator is love (romantic, brotherly, or unconditional). If you love the other person, you would be willing to make some sacrifices to reconcile. Look inward to understand your responsibility for the separation. Forgive the other person's role. Show empathy, compassion, and remorse for your role in the disagreement. Then reach out, in love, to do the restoration work.

I understand that there are many people who have been hurt to such a degree that attempting to reconcile, especially if the other person does not express remorse, would cause them even more pain. Some individuals would take advantage of the opportunity of a repaired relationship and create additional suffering. In other cases, a repaired relationship might not be appropriate or open a new can of worms. Use your judgment and your heart to make the decision when deciding to reconcile. You can still free your heart through forgiveness without bringing the other person back into your life.

Reconciliation Letter Template

Dear_____,

   I miss you (expound upon why you miss them)

_____ .

   Over the last (weeks, months, years), I have learned

_____ .

   Our relationship is more important than any disagreement between us.

Can we meet for (coffee, tea, dinner, lunch, phone call)?
With (warm regards, best wishes, love)
Your name (informal name)

Reconciliation Letter Tips

Start by telling the person how much you value your relationship. Express your gratitude for having this person in your life.

No need to blame anyone, but express your remorse over your part in the disagreement if appropriate. You don't have to be in the wrong to reconcile; remember, the goal is to build a harmonious relationship. Keep your tone gracious and humble. Oversee your words, and don't include hidden agendas or trigger comments.

Look for a solution, such as avoiding a topic that causes dissent. Agree to disagree.

Restate your desire to heal the relationship and how much you value the person.

Reconciliation Quotes for Inspiration:

"Reconciliation is more beautiful than victory."
—Violeta Chamorro

"It is much safer to reconcile an enemy than to conquer him; victory may deprive him of his poison, but reconciliation of his will."
—Owen Feltham

"Reconciliation is a decision that you take in your heart."
—Ingrid Betancourt

Reconciliation Words

Love, appreciate, worthy, esteem, treasure, prize, significant, cherish, value, admire, virtue, revere, honor, venerate, I hold you in high regard, hold dear, beloved dear one, adore, eminent, invaluable, self-sacrificing, kind, warm-hearted, kind-hearted, caring, sensitive, loving, dependable, tender, considerate, benevolent, generous, friendly, courteous, warmhearted, good-natured, magnanimous, gentle, unselfish, selfless, inclusive.

Remorse, deep regret, sadness, apologies, I apologize, regret, guilt, guilty conscience, a pang of conscience, heartache, broken-hearted, misery, distress, remorse, embarrassment, self-reproof, atonement, concern.

Resolution, key, benefit, settlement, way out, brainstorm, answer, cure, remedy, compromise, reconcile, understanding, conclude, patch up, conciliate, work out, make right, come to terms, satisfy, handle, reach an agreement, meet in the middle, settling, mediate, find a solution, breakthrough, antidote, alleviate.

Heal, restore, mend, rehabilitate, recover, getting over the hill, strengthen, reconcile, relieve the pain, make better, revive, love, appreciate (back to the first group of love words to end on a high note!)

Resources:

https://morinholistictherapy.com/reconciling-with-estranged
    -family/

https://www.verywellfamily.com/how-to-rekindle-a-relationship
    -with-estranged-family-4796333

https://onlinegrad.pepperdine.edu/blog/reconnection-family
    -estrangement-forgiveness/

https://www.usip.org/issue-areas/reconciliation

Apology Letters

Apologizing does not always mean you're wrong
and the other person is right. It just means you
value your relationship more than your ego.
—*Mark Matthews*

None of us are perfect, and we all make mistakes. Unfortunately, at least in the US, I believe that we are addicted to being right, and we are too frequently offended. Both of these attributes can lead to problems and can lead us to do things that hurt others. Giving grace and forgiveness to others is a beautiful gift that can free us from our negative feelings. One of my dear friends in Rwanda (see The Legacy of Peace) told me that forgiveness is like the metamorphosis of a butterfly. You start out with anger or resentment that resembles the characteristics of an ugly caterpillar always eating things up. Through the process of forgiveness, you change into a beautiful butterfly free of the earth and able to fly to the heavens. The people in Rwanda know about forgiveness!

One of the most important things we can teach our children is to understand that they are sometimes wrong, and it is essential to recognize when they are wrong and make things right.

The first step in making things right is to apologize. The best time to apologize is immediately and in person. If that chance passes you by and you are uncomfortable talking about the situation, a written apology will do the trick. Understand that an apology doesn't guarantee forgiveness, but it surely increases the chances, and you will have the peace of knowing that you have done your part.

Written apologies are particularly helpful if the situation is very emotional or if the person you are apologizing to is so hurt that they may respond uncomfortably. Written apologies can be in email form, but the most personal is a letter, preferably hand-written (if you have legible handwriting).

According to *Psychology Today*, there are three parts to an effective apology: acknowledgment, remorse and empathy, and restitution.

To express remorse, you might say that you regret what happened or wish for another outcome. If you feel you did something wrong, you might say you are sorry for your actions. Expressing sadness at the loss of the relationship is another way to express remorse.

Empathy means that you put yourself in the shoes of the other person. One of the best ways to express empathy is to openly listen or think carefully about how the other person must feel and validate those feelings. Using words like, "You must feel so (unhappy, betrayed, sad, angry)" will help the other person understand that you care about them.

Restitution means to give back or restore. If there is some-thing you can do to make the wrong right, do it! Sometimes, especially when your words hurt someone else, letting them know that you are sorry you let those words out and that you did not mean them is all you can do.

Need help getting your apology letter started? Here are some tips and words that may be useful!

First of all, let go of your ego. Make sure your tone is respect-ful, courteous, and thoughtful; humility is the key. Show your love for this person as a fellow human being.

Make sure all the apology parts are included:

Acknowledgment
Admit your mistake, simply, with no excuses.

Remorse and Empathy
Describe how you may have made that person feel.
Describe how the realization that you caused him or her pain made you feel.
What have you learned?
Why you won't do this again.

Restitution
What you will do to make things better and show your remorse.

Ask for Forgiveness
Asking for forgiveness is important. Forgive them for any part they may have played, but don't mention this in the letter unless they have asked for forgiveness, as telling them you forgive them weakens your apology to them by highlighting the wrongs they committed.

Realize that the other person may not forgive you. Knowing that you are offering a sincere apology and doing what you can to make things right should give you some peace. You can't control the behavior of others. Apologizing, like forgiveness, can set you free.

Apology letter template
Dear_____,

I am so sorry that I (no excuses, you are just sorry) _____

_____

You must have felt (or I can't imagine how you felt) _____

_____

_____

_____

I feel _____

_____

_____

*I know now that*_____

_____

_____

_____

I will never do this again.
Can you forgive me?
With (warm regards, love, gratitude)
Your name (informal)

Apology Quotes for Inspiration

> *"Never forget the nine most important words of any*
> *family-I love you. You are beautiful. Please forgive me."*
> — *H. Jackson Brown Jr.*

> *"Chocolate says 'I'm sorry' so much better than words."*
> —*Rachel Vincent, My Soul to Save*

(Works for me!)

Words and Phrases That May Help You Write

Respect, esteem, honor, admiration, admire, value, prizes, adore, accept, love, recognize, you matter to me, thoughtfulness, honoring, acknowledge, courteous, beloved, dear one, cherish, appreciate, tenderness, sweet, treasure, I value our relationship, kindness, dependability, conscientious, enthusiastic.

Regret, guilt, repentance, grief, sorry, penitence, guilt, pangs of conscience, sadness, heartbreak, distress, misery, regret, deep regret, heartache, heartbreak, misery, sorry, anxiety, embarrassment, apology, agony, self-reproof, broken heart, worry, trouble, misgiving, repenting, suffering, concern, dejection, despair.

Restitution, restoration, amends, recompense, repayment, recovery, payment, regain, reinstate, atonement, rehabilitate, settlement, re-establish, penance, recover, remedy, damage, squaring things, offsetting, recompense, restitute, compensation, relief, remediate, surrender, recapture, recoup, repair, compensate.

Pardon, excuse me, release, free, have mercy, please accept my apology, please be merciful, grant me amnesty, have sympathy, I want the best for you.

Resources:

https://www.npr.org/2023/01/25/1150972343/how-to-say-
   sorry-give-good-apology
https://www.mindtools.com/afhit60/how-to-apologize
https://www.health.harvard.edu/blog/the-art-of-a-heartfelt
   -apology-2021041322366

You Can Do This!

I know that the recommendations I have in this book may seem daunting. Remember, you don't have to do them all (although a will and health care directive would be a good start). I vowed to my family that I would not publish this book until I have completed or started all of the steps that I chose to do on the Death Preppers Checklist. Some of these will be in continual progress, such as the adventure books for my grandchildren, and many will require periodic updating as life changes.

Many of us are great at getting things done alone. I wish I had that gift. I am a procrastinator. It took writing this book and the associated accountability to get my tasks completed. I also brought in my book club, my church, and my accountability partner, Terri Hands, to help. It turned out to be a fun project, especially helping people with their legacy stories.

Do you have a book club, church group, or other collection of like-minded people who would benefit from working as a group to "get their affairs in order?" If so, you can work on your tasks together. Back in the 1990s, there was an entire industry associated with creating "Memory Books." I know because I fell right into that movement. The result was that my children have beautiful memory books focusing on their amazingness, as seen through my eyes. I am now using the boxes and boxes of art supplies accumulated during that period to make my adventure books for my grandchildren. For those who did not invest in stickers, art punches, special pencils, and beautiful paper, you can create your legacy/adventure books easily on your computer. There are many companies that will help you make your books if you choose to do that.

So, if you are reading this, high five to me for being up to date on my legacy project and high five to you for getting started.

My ultimate goal is that when I die, those who survive me will be better off because I lived and can thrive in a world without me. My most important legacy is the love I have for them. Everybody can leave a legacy of love. I hope this book helps you to live the rest of your life with extraordinary focus and prepare those dearest to you for a life full of happiness and joy in your memory.

Appendix

Appendix One

Legacy Recipes

Grandma Harms' Lefse

Grandma Harms made this lefse for almost every family gathering. We remember her on Christmas morning when we make lefse for breakfast. This lefse tradition ensures that everyone wakes up early, Those who snooze lose!

8 cups mashed potatoes (riced or fresh mashed work best, but in a pinch, you can use instant)
1 stick butter
½ cup heavy cream
1 tsp. salt
4 cups flour

Mix the potatoes, cream, butter, and salt. Beat well and cool. Add 4 cups flour and mix together until a dough forms. Roll dough into a ball the size of a tennis ball. You may have to add some flour to keep it from sticking. Refrigerate. Take 3-4 balls out at a time and roll out the dough until it is thin enough to lift up without breaking. Place on a griddle and cook until bubbles form, and the underside is light brown. Turn over and cook the other side. Place lefse between towels to keep warm. Fill and roll.

Traditional Harms Lefse: Spread with soft butter and sprinkle with brown sugar.

Traditional variations: Spread with butter and sprinkle with granulated white sugar or brown sugar or sugar and cinnamon.

Non-Traditional Lefse: Place ham and cheese, turkey and cheese (maybe a little cranberry sauce), or other savory combination onto lefse.
Roll the lefse like a jelly roll and cut it into four sections. If making savory lefse, microwave to melt the cheese. ENJOY!

Aunt Theda's Chocolate Cake with Caramel Frosting

2 cups flour
1 ¾ cup sugar
1 egg
1 tbsp. baking soda
⅔ cup oil
1 cup buttermilk
½ cup cocoa
1 cup hot coffee
½ tsp. salt

Mix all ingredients (except for coffee) and beat in a large bowl. Beat in coffee.
Pour into a 9 x13 pan and bake for 30 minutes at 350-degree oven.

Caramel frosting

¼ cup butter
2 tbsp. milk
1 tsp. vanilla
½ cup brown sugar
1 cup powdered sugar

Melt butter, stir in brown sugar, and cook until bubbly. Add milk and bring to a boil. Add vanilla, remove from heat, and beat in powdered sugar.

Aunt Judy's Best-Ever Angel Food Cake with Burnt Butter Icing

1 ½ cups egg whites (approx. one dozen)
1 ½ tsp. cream of tartar
⅓ tsp. salt
1 ½ tsp. vanilla
½ tsp. almond extract
1 cup sugar
1 cup cake flour
1 1/2 cup powdered sugar
Brown Butter Frosting
½ cup butter
3 cups powdered sugar
3 tbsp. cream

Put sugar, egg whites, cream of tartar, salt, vanilla, and almond extract in a large mixing bowl and beat until stiff. Do not under beat! Mix in cake flour and powdered sugar. Pour into a tube pan. Bake at 375 degrees F for 35-40 minutes.

Brown Butter Icing

Melt and brown ½ cup butter, cool. Add 3 cups powdered sugar, add 3 tbsp. cream. Beat together until smooth.

Mrs. Brown's Carrot Cake

2 ½ cups flour
2 tsp. cinnamon
1 tsp. baking soda
½ tsp. salt
2 cups sugar
1 cup oil
2 cups grated carrots
3 eggs
1 cup walnuts
1 cup drained crushed pineapple
1 ½ tsp. vanilla

Sift dry ingredients together and add remaining ingredients. Beat for 3 minutes. Bake in a greased and floured tube pan at 270 degrees for 1 hour and 15 minutes. If you use a flat pan, bake at 350 degrees for 35-45 minutes. Test with toothpick for doneness. (Toothpick should come out clean).

Sandy Abraham's Cream Cheese Frosting

3 cups powdered sugar
¼ tsp. salt
1 tsp. vanilla
1 tsp. butter flavoring
1 8 oz. package cream cheese

Blend in mixer.
Add 1 cup Crisco to the mixture and beat on high speed for 5-10 minutes until fluffy.

Appendix Two

Legacy Letter Resource: Useful Legacy, Gratitude, and Reconciliation Quotes from the Number One Bestselling Book of All Time (The Bible, Over 5 Billion Sold)

This appendix is designed to help those who are writing legacy, gratitude, or reconciliation letters by giving some quotes and words that may be useful in inspiring them to write. There is wisdom here for both Christians and non-Christians.

GRATITUDE
Philippians 4:6-7
Do not be anxious about anything, but in everything by prayer and supplication with thanksgiving let your requests be made known to God. And the peace of God, which surpasses all understanding, will guard your hearts and your minds in Christ Jesus.

2 Corinthians 4:15
All this is for your benefit, so that the grace that is reaching more and more people may cause thanksgiving to overflow to the glory of God.

James 1:17
Every good gift and every perfect gift is from above, coming down from the Father of lights with whom there is no variation or shadow due to change.

1 Thessalonians 5:18
Be thankful in all circumstances, for this is God's will for you
who belong to Christ Jesus.

1 Thessalonians 5:16-18
Rejoice always, pray without ceasing, give thanks in all circumstances; for this is the will of God in Christ Jesus for you.

Corinthians 15:57
But thanks be to God! He gives us the victory through our Lord
Jesus Christ.

Ephesians 1:16
I have not stopped giving thanks for you, remembering you in
my prayers.

Isaiah 41:10
Fear not, for I am with you; be not dismayed, for I am your God;
I will strengthen you, I will help you, I will uphold you with my
righteous right hand.

1 Chronicles 16:34
Give thanks to the Lord, for He is good; His love endures forever.

Colossians 3:15
Let the peace of Christ rule in your hearts, since as members of
one body you were called to peace. And be thankful.

2 Thessalonians 1:3
We ought always to give thanks to God for you, brothers, as is
right, because your faith is growing abundantly, and the love of
every one of you for one another is increasing.

2 Corinthians 9:15
Thanks be to God for his inexpressible gift.

Matthew 5:16
Let your light so shine before men, that they may see your good works, and glorify your Father, which is in heaven.

Colossians 4:2
Devote yourself to prayer, being watchful and thankful.

1 Timothy 4:4-5
For everything God created is good, and nothing is to be rejected if it is received with thanksgiving, because it is consecrated by the word of God and prayer.

John 3:16
For God so loved the world that He gave His only son, that whoever believes in Him should not perish but have eternal life.

Psalm 95:2
Let us come into His presence with thanksgiving; let us make a joyful noise to Him with songs of praise!

Psalm 9:1
I will give thanks to you, Lord, with all my heart; I will tell of all your wonderful deeds.

1 Corinthians 1:4
I give thanks to my God always for you because of the grace of God that was given you in Christ Jesus.

James 1:17
Every good gift and every perfect gift is from above, coming down from the Father of lights with whom there is no variation or shadow due to change.

Psalm 118:24
This is the day that the Lord has made, let us rejoice and be glad in it.

Acts 24:3
In every way and everywhere we accept this with all gratitude.

Psalm 110:4
Enter His gates with thanksgiving, and His courts with praise! Give thanks to Him; bless His name!

Proverbs 15:30
A cheerful look brings joy to the heart, and good news gives health to the bones.

1 Corinthians 12:4
There are different kinds of gifts, but the same spirit distributes them.

Matthew 6:21
For where your treasure is, there your heart will be also.

Ephesians 5:20
Giving thanks always and for everything to God the father in the name of our Lord Jesus Christ.

Daniel 2:23

To you, oh God of my fathers, I give thanks and praise, for you have given me wisdom and power.

LEGACY
John 3:16
For God so loved the world that He gave His only son, that whoever believes in Him should not perish but have eternal life.

Romans 8:38-39
For I am convinced that neither death nor life, neither angels nor demons, neither the present nor the future, nor any powers, neither height nor depth, nor anything else in all creation, will be able to separate us from the love of God that is in Christ Jesus our Lord.

Jeremiah 29:11
"For I know the plans I have for you," declares the Lord, "plans to prosper you and not to harm you, plans to give you hope and a future."

Chronicles 16:8
Oh give thanks to the Lord; call upon His name; make known His deeds among the peoples!

Psalm 76:4
You are resplendent with light, more majestic than mountains rich with game.

Matthew 11:28
Come to me, all who labor and are heavy laden, and I will give you rest.

Psalm 50:20
The one who offers thanksgiving as his sacrifice glorifies me; to one who orders his way rightly I will show the salvation of God!

Colossians 3:15
And let the peace of Christ rule in your hearts, to which indeed you were called in the one body. And be thankful.

Psalm 28:7
The Lord is my strength and my shield; in Him my heart trusts, and I am helped; my heart exults, and with my song I give thanks to Him.

Psalm 23:1-6
The Lord is my shepherd; I shall not want. He maketh me to lie down in green pastures: He leadeth me beside the still waters. He restoreth my soul: He leads me in the paths of righteousness for His name's sake. Yea, though I walk through the valley of the shadow of death, I will fear no evil; for you are with me; your rod and your staff, they comfort me. You prepare a table before me in the presence of my enemies; you anoint my head with oil; My cup runs over. Surely goodness and mercy shall follow me all the days of my life; and I will dwell in the house of the Lord Forever.

Colossians 3:17
And whatever you do, whether in word or deed, do it all in the name of the Lord Jesus, giving thanks to God the Father through him.

Ruth 2:12

The Lord repay you for what you have done, and a full reward be given you by the Lord, the God of Israel, under whose wings you have come to take refuge!

2 Corinthians 4:16

So we do not lose heart. Though our outer self is wasting away, our inner self is being renewed day by day.

1 Peter 1:7

These have come so that the proven genuineness of your faith–of greater worth than gold, which perishes even through refined by fire–may result in praise, glory, and honor when Jesus Christ is revealed.

Psalm 107:8-9

Let them give thanks to the Lord for His unfailing love and His wonderful deeds for mankind, for He satisfies the thirsty and fills the hungry with good things.

Romans 8:28

And we know that for those who love God all things work together for good, for those who are called according to His purpose.

Matthew 13:16

But blessed are your eyes because they see, and your ears because they hear.

Hebrews 13:15

Through Him then let us continually offer up a sacrifice of praise to God, that is, the fruit of lips that acknowledge His name.

2 Corinthians 9:11
You will be enriched in every way to be generous in every way, which through us will produce thanksgiving to God.

1 Timothy 4:12
Don't let anyone look down on you because you are young, but set an example for the believers in speech, in conduct, in love, in faith, and in purity.

Colossians 3:2
Set your minds on things above, not on earthly things.

Deuteronomy 31:6
Be strong and courageous. Do not be afraid or terrified because of them, for the Lord your God goes with you; He will never leave you nor forsake you."

Isaiah 43:19
See, I am doing a new thing! Now it springs up; do you not perceive it? I am making a way in the wilderness and streams in the wasteland.

Isaiah 58:11
The Lord will guide you always; He will satisfy your needs in a sun-scorched land and will strengthen your frame. You will be like a well-watered garden, like a spring whose waters never fail.

Matthew 5:16
In the same way, let your light shine before others, that they may see your good deeds and glorify your Father in heaven.

Philippians 1:6
Being confident of this, that he who began a good work in you will carry it on to completion until the day of Christ Jesus.

Psalm 119:10
I seek you with all my heart; do not let me stray from your commands.

Psalm 16:7-11
I will praise the Lord, who counsels me; even at night my heart instructs me. I keep my eyes always on the Lord. With Him at my right hand, I will not be shaken. Therefore my heart is glad and my tongue rejoices; my body also will rest secure, because you will not abandon me to the realm of the dead, nor will you let your faithful one see decay. You make known to me the path of life; you will fill me with joy in your presence, with eternal pleasures at your right hand.

Psalm 20:4
May He give you the desire of your heart and make all your plans succeed.

Romans 12:2
Do not conform to the pattern of this world, but be transformed by the renewing of your mind. Then you will be able to test and approve what God's will is—his good, pleasing and perfect will.

Deuteronomy 31:8
The Lord himself goes before you and will be with you; He will never leave you nor forsake you. Do not be afraid; do not be discouraged.

Proverbs 2
My son, if you accept my words and store up my commands within you, turning your ear to wisdom and applying your heart to understanding— indeed, if you call out for insight and cry aloud for understanding, and if you look for it as for silver and search for it as for hidden treasure, then you will understand the fear of the Lord and find the knowledge of God. For the Lord gives wisdom; from his mouth come knowledge and understanding. He holds success in store for the upright, He is a shield to those whose walk is blameless, for He guards the course of the just and protects the way of His faithful ones. Then you will understand what is right and just and fair—every good path. For wisdom will enter your heart, and knowledge will be pleasant to your soul. Discretion will protect you, and understanding will guard you. Wisdom will save you from the ways of wicked men, from men whose words are perverse, who have left the straight paths to walk in dark ways, who delight in doing wrong and rejoice in the perverseness of evil, whose paths are crooked and who are devious in their ways. Wisdom will save you also from the adulterous woman, from the wayward woman with her seductive words, who has left the partner of her youth and ignored the covenant she made before God. Surely her house leads down to death and her paths to the spirits of the dead. None who go to her return or attain the paths of life. Thus you will walk in the ways of the good and keep to the paths of the righteous. For the upright will live in the land, and the blameless will remain in it; but the wicked will be cut off from the land, and the unfaithful will be torn from it.

Isaiah 26:3-4
You will keep in perfect peace those whose minds are steadfast, because they trust in you. Trust in the Lord forever, for the Lord, the Lord himself, is the Rock eternal.

Psalm 119:31-32
I hold fast to your statutes, Lord; do not let me be put to shame. I run in the path of your commands, for you have broadened my understanding.

Isaiah 40:29-31
He gives strength to the weary and increases the power of the weak. Even youths grow tired and weary, and young men stumble and fall; but those who hope in the Lord will renew their strength. They will soar on wings like eagles; they will run and not grow weary, they will walk and not be faint.

Psalm 119:105-106
Your word is a lamp for my feet, a light on my path. I have taken an oath and confirmed it, that I will follow your righteous laws.

1 Corinthians 1:4-9
I always thank my God for you because of His grace given you in Christ Jesus. For in Him you have been enriched in every way— with all kinds of speech and with all knowledge— God thus confirming our testimony about Christ among you. Therefore you do not lack any spiritual gift as you eagerly wait for our Lord Jesus Christ to be revealed. He will also keep you firm to the end, so that you will be blameless on the day of our Lord Jesus Christ. God is faithful, who has called you into fellowship with his Son, Jesus Christ our Lord.

Proverbs 4
Listen, my sons, to a father's instruction; pay attention and gain understanding. I give you sound learning, so do not forsake my teaching. For I too was a son to my father, still tender, and cherished by my mother. Then He taught me, and

He said to me, "Take hold of my words with all your heart; keep my commands, and you will live. Get wisdom, get understanding; do not forget my words or turn away from them. Do not forsake wisdom, and she will protect you; love her, and she will watch over you. The beginning of wisdom is this: Get wisdom. Though it cost all you have, get understanding. Cherish her, and she will exalt you; embrace her, and she will honor you. She will give you a garland to grace your head and present you with a glorious crown. Listen, my son, accept what I say, and the years of your life will be many. I instruct you in the way of wisdom and lead you along straight paths. When you walk, your steps will not be hampered; when you run, you will not stumble. Hold on to instruction, do not let it go; guard it well, for it is your life. Do not set foot on the path of the wicked or walk in the way of evildoers. Avoid it, do not travel on it; turn from it and go on your way. For they cannot rest until they do evil; they are robbed of sleep till they make someone stumble. They eat the bread of wickedness and drink the wine of violence. The path of the righteous is like the morning sun, shining ever brighter till the full light of day. But the way of the wicked is like deep darkness; they do not know what makes them stumble. My son, pay attention to what I say; turn your ear to my words. Do not let them out of your sight, keep them within your heart; for they are life to those who find them and health to one's whole body. Above all else, guard your heart, for everything you do flows from it. Keep your mouth free of perversity; keep corrupt talk far from your lips. Let your eyes look straight ahead; fix your gaze directly before you. Give careful thought to the paths for your feet and be steadfast in all your ways. Do not turn to the right or the left; keep your foot from evil.

Proverbs 23:17-18

Do not let your heart envy sinners, but always be zealous for the fear of the Lord. There is surely a future hope for you, and your hope will not be cut off.

Proverbs 24:14

Know also that wisdom is like honey for you: If you find it, there is a future hope for you, and your hope will not be cut off.

Psalm 27:14

Wait for the Lord; be strong and take heart and wait for the Lord.

RECONCILIATION

Please be careful in writing your letter not to place blame on the other person. Although reconciliation does involve forgiveness, it also involves giving grace. Give love and grace to them as Jesus gave to us and let God be the judge!

Hebrews 12:14

Make every effort to live in peace with everyone and to be holy; without holiness no one will see the Lord.

Colossians 3:13

Bear with each other and forgive one another if any of you has a grievance against someone. Forgive as the Lord forgave you.

Ephesians 4:32

Be kind and compassionate to one another, forgiving each other, just as in Christ God forgave you.

Luke 23:34
Jesus said, "Father, forgive them, for they do not know what they are doing." And they divided up his clothes by casting lots.

Matthew 5:24
Leave your gift there in front of the altar. First go and be reconciled to them; then come and offer your gift.

Romans 5:10
For if, while we were God's enemies, we were reconciled to Him through the death of His Son, how much more, having been reconciled, shall we be saved through His life!

Romans 11:15
For if their rejection brought reconciliation to the world, what will their acceptance be but life from the dead?

Romans 12:1-2
Therefore, I urge you, brothers and sisters, in view of God's mercy, to offer your bodies as a living sacrifice, holy and pleasing to God—this is your true and proper worship. Do not conform to the pattern of this world, but be transformed by the renewing of your mind. Then you will be able to test and approve what God's will is—his good, pleasing and perfect will.

Colossians 1:20-22
And through Him to reconcile to himself all things, whether things on Earth or things in heaven, by making peace through His blood, shed on the cross. Once you were alienated from God and were enemies in your minds because of your evil behavior. But now He has reconciled you by Christ's physical

body through death to present you holy in His sight, without blemish and free from accusation.

2 Corinthians 5:18-21
All this is from God, who reconciled us to himself through Christ and gave us the ministry of reconciliation: that God was reconciling the world to himself in Christ, not counting people's sins against them. And He has committed to us the message of reconciliation. We are therefore Christ's ambassadors, as though God were making His appeal through us. We implore you on Christ's behalf: Be reconciled to God. God made Him who had no sin to be sin for us, so that in Him we might become the righteousness of God.

Ephesians 2:15-18
By setting aside in His flesh the law with its commands and regulations. His purpose was to create in himself one new humanity out of the two, thus making peace, and in one body to reconcile both of them to God through the cross, by which He put to death their hostility. He came and preached peace to you who were far away and peace to those who were near. For through Him we both have access to the Father by one Spirit.

Ephesians 1:3-10
Praise be to the God and Father of our Lord Jesus Christ, who has blessed us in the heavenly realms with every spiritual blessing in Christ. For He chose us in Him before the creation of the world to be holy and blameless in His sight. In love He predestined us for adoption to sonship through Jesus Christ, in accordance with His pleasure and will— to the praise of His glorious grace, which He has freely given us in the One He loves. In Him we have redemption through His blood, the forgiveness of sins, in accordance with

the riches of God's grace that He lavished on us. With all wisdom and understanding, He made known to us the mystery of His will according to His good pleasure, which He purposed in Christ, to be put into effect when the times reach their fulfillment—to bring unity to all things in heaven and on Earth under Christ.

USEFUL WORDS

Love, affection, beloved, dear, adore, cherish, appreciate, admire, high regard, respect, friendship, sweet, dearest, warmth, treasure, relationship, endearment, delight, kind, hold dear, loyal, angel, compassion, enthusiastic, goodwill, warm regards, companionship, fellowship, harmony, camaraderie, affinity, empathy, sympathy, brotherhood, sisterhood, goodwill, congenial, solidarity, fraternity, understanding, kindness, tenderness, support, mutual support, kinship, like-mindedness, geniality, connection, affiliation, good nature, rapport, feeling, sensitivity, closeness, like-mindedness, congeniality, sensibility, compatibility, considerate, insight, warm-heartedness, brotherly love, sisterly love, love in Christ, trustworthiness, reliable, constancy, stability, authenticity, responsibility, steadfastness, devotion, integrity, dedicated, character, high principles, high mindedness, virtue, faith, worthy, justness, sincere, good faith, noble, obedient to God, openhearted, peace, truce, conciliation, agreement, understanding, reuniting, amity, conciliation, peace offering, make up, forgiveness, mercy, grace, restoration, compassion, adorn, mercy, blessing, goodwill, pardon, charity, thanks, preciousness, generosity, kindliness, decency, honor, benevolence, courtesy, graciousness, helpfulness, loveliness, fineness, goodness, holiness, pardon, indulgence, forbearance, charity, mercies, magnanimity, patience, toleration, understanding, lifesavers, soft-heartedness, tenderness, altruism, equanimity, fruit of the spirit, humility, holiness, selflessness, humble, gentleness, unselfishness, surrender to God, acceptance of God's plan.

About the Author

Dr. Kimberly Harms has been around the block in life! She has served as a Commissioned Officer in the United States Public Health Service, a dental school professor, a grief counselor, a death doula, a civil mediator, a clinical dentist with her late husband, Jim, in Farmington Minnesota, a school board Chair, President of an international women's organization, the first woman President of the Minnesota Dental Association, a national spokesperson for the American Dental Association, an award-winning, bestselling author and international speaker. She has also suffered many personal losses. Her most important role is as a mother to her two surviving children and grandmother to 6 precious grandchildren.